HOW TO MAKE 100

Paper Flowers

Ideas and Instruction for Folding, Cutting, and Simple Sculptures

Maria Noble

Creative Publishing
international

Creative Publishing
international

First published in the United States of America by
Creative Publishing international, Inc., a member of
Quayside Publishing Group
400 First Avenue North
Suite 400
Minneapolis, MN 55401
1-800-328-3895
www.creativepub.com

ISBN: 978-1-58923-751-3

10 9 8 7 6 5 4 3 2

Library of Congress Cataloging-in-Publication Data available

Copy Editor: Catherine Broberg
Proofreader: Jessica Best
Design: Creative Publishing international
Illustrations: Mattie Reposa
Photographs: Maria Noble

Printed in China

To St. Jude,
and to my parents

Contents

Origami Blossoms

Quilled Florals

Introduction

Making paper flowers is a multifaceted art—the culmination of a rich and varied history filled with artisans who perfected many methods to arrive at the beautiful results.

The art of making paper flowers is believed to have originated from China almost 2,000 years ago. From Asia the art spread to the Americas via Spanish ships arriving in Mexico. Its popularity surged immensely during Colonial times, especially for decorating Christian churches. In Victorian days, women adorned their homes with paper flowers when the real ones were out of season. As the popularity of the craft grew, hobbyists became artisans, passing their skills down to future generations.

My passion for paper flowers was ignited early by my mother and aunt, who loved fashioning innovative arrangements from all types of fabric and paper. Although as an adult, I initially worked in the computer field, it was during my time as a stay-at-home mom that I returned to my roots and began to explore the art that had surrounded and captivated me as a child. I incorporated memories with my own research and experimentation to bring my new ideas to life.

What began as a hobby soon bloomed into an online store, St. Jude's Creations (www.stjudescreations.com), where clients can now custom order flowers for home décor, weddings, and other events.

It has been an amazing journey, exploring and expanding this unique craft passed down to me by my mother. In this book, I have distilled my years of experience to share with you the pleasure and fulfillment of paper flowers. I have also included origami and quilled flowers to showcase the myriad possibilities that can be achieved with a diversity of techniques and materials.

The projects and techniques presented in this book are designed to help you learn to sculpt 100 different types of paper flowers. Step-by-step instructions and easy-to-follow photos will get you creating pieces that are remarkably simple yet elegant enough for any occasion.

Use paper flowers for a variety of creative applications. Enhance your home's personality in a way that store-bought flowers cannot. Display them in vases or on wreaths. Make an eclectic, modern arrangement or pot them like the real thing. Give thoughtful gifts, and stage awesome craft projects for kids. Create a bridal bouquet that doubles as a lasting memento to be treasured for years to come. There are so many designs and uses yet to be imagined. I hope the ideas in this book can inspire you, the way those childhood crafting sessions inspired me, to design and create new flowers on your own.

Maria Noble

Materials and Tools

Paper

I have created the flowers in this book using all different types of paper to demonstrate the versatility of the medium. You can purchase a wide variety of decorative papers at your local art or craft store, but many of them can be commonly found at home and recycled.

CREPE PAPER

Crêpe paper is tissue paper that has been coated with sizing (a glue-like substance) and then creped (creased in a way similar to party streamers) to create gathers which are called grains. They come in many varieties and an array of colors. Always keep the grain vertical while cutting templates out of crepe paper.

Crepe paper folds. These are single-ply crepe paper sheets, 20" x 7.5 ft. (59 cm x 1.75 m), folded into a narrow, flat bundle. They are found at art and craft stores and sometimes party supply stores. They come in an assortment of gorgeous colors and are very pliable. This is the thinnest type of crepe paper available.

Doublette crepe paper. This duplex crepe paper is made from two pieces of tightly-grained crepe paper which have been firmly glued together to create a stiffer material. Made with 135% stretch, the two-ply craft crepe paper is easy to work with and will hold its shape when formed into petals, leaves, or any design you can imagine. Folded duplex crepe paper sheets measure 9 ¾" inches wide by 49" long (25 cm x 125 cm).These are mostly found in online stores (see sources, page 00)

Florist crepe. At 180 grams, this paper looks and feels more like a sturdy fabric. It is available in a selection of beautiful, rich colors and is sold in rolls. These are mostly found in online stores.

Crepe paper streamers. These are similar to crepe paper folds except that they are precut into 1½" to 2" (3.8 to 5 cm) wide strips and rolled. They are sold as party streamers and can be purchased in many craft, party and even dollar stores. Alternatively, you can cut crepe paper folds across the grain at 2" (5 cm) width to get a streamer roll.

SCRAPBOOK PAPER

Popular among scrapbook enthusiasts, this paper comes in a variety of prints and colors. Sheets typically measure 12" x 12" (30.5 x 20.5 cm) and come in various thicknesses. They may be sold loose or in pads or are available at all craft stores.

Cardstock ranges from a heavy thickness to very light weight. The lightweight sheets are pliable, with one side patterned and the other plain white. Sturdier scrapbook paper, also called cardstock, is usually double sided.

CONSTRUCTION PAPER

Construction paper (sugar paper) is a tough, coarse, colored paper. The texture is slightly rough, and the surface unfinished. One of the defining features of construction paper is the radiance of its colors. Construction paper is put to many and varied uses, including cutting and pasting projects and projects that involve drawing, sketching, or coloring and is widely used in elementary schools.

PAPER NAPKINS

These are simply the common paper napkins you might find around the house or at most stores in the party goods section. They come plain and in patterns, with the patterned varieties tending to be thicker.

ORIGAMI PAPER

Origami paper is paper used for the Japanese art of paper folding. There are many varieties of lightweight, decorative paper designed specifically for origami, but the only real requirement of this medium is that it must be able to hold a crease. Light weight scrapbook paper could be repurposed for origami, as well.

Kami or koi origami paper is widely available and inexpensive. Kami is thin and easy to fold. It is usually printed only on one side, with a solid color or pattern. These patterns can be as simple as a gradation from red to blue, or as complex as a multi-colored kimono pattern of flowers and cranes with gold foil embellishments. Kami comes in several sizes, but standard sizes include 75 × 75 mm (about 3 × 3 inches), 6-inch squares and 10-inch squares.

QUILLING PAPER STRIPS

Quilling paper is available on the consumer market in over 250 colors and dimensions. It can be divided into various categories, including solid colored quilling paper, graduated, two-tone, and acid free. It is available in various sizes, including ⅛", ¼" and ⅜" (3, 6, and 10 mm) widths. Furthermore, you can create quilling strips by cutting lightweight paper.

RECYCLED PAPER

Don't discount found materials—sometimes the makings of the most inventive flowers can be found in unconventional places. Keep an eye out for striking junk mail, or extra wrapping paper. Other examples include everything from newspapers and flyers to paper bags and brightly colored catalogs. Those glossy mailers and eye-catching flyers can be perfect both for your own projects and for kids' craft activities.

Glue

Use a tacky, quick drying glue. Any glue that is thicker and dries quickly and clear can be used.

Florist Wire

Use 22- to 26-gauge aluminum wire to tie flowers. This can be found in most craft stores.

Stem Wire

Use 18 gauge stem wire when bundling strands of wire together to form stronger stems. Use brown paper wound stem wire or dowels to support large heavier flowers.

Florist Tape

This wax-infused, self-sealing finishing tape is useful for attaching together the stems of flowers and leaves while finishing the wires with a realistic look. As you slightly stretch the tape and wrap it in a spiral around the stem, the warmth of your fingers melts the wax so the tape sticks to itself. Florists use it to secure wires to real flower stems so they can be manipulated into new designs. Florist tape can be found in most craft stores.

Bamboo Skewers

Use these for curling the ends of petals. They can be found in most grocery stores by the barbecue supplies.

Stamens

Make your flowers look realistic with decorative stamens, sold in craft and floral supply stores. These tiny colored ball- or oat-shaped ends are connected in pairs by covered florist wire, and are often used by sugar artists to finish icing flowers on cakes. They are sold in small bundles and are available in many colors and sizes. If you cannot find your desired color, use paint to color the stamens, allowing to dry before use.

Scissors

You'll need sharp scissors for cutting out petals and leaves. Use a smaller pair for cutting out smaller flowers and fringes. Stainless steel scissors work well for intricate cuts.

PINKING SHEARS

Use to trim zigzag edges for petals and leaves.

SHAPED-BLADE SCISSORS

Available in many styles, the blades on these craft scissors are scalloped, wavy, notched, or otherwise shaped. Use them to trim decorative edges for petals and leaves.

Wire Cutter

Use to cut stem wires and florist wire.

Pencils

Use to trace out the templates on thick cardstock paper. Mark templates and store separately for reuse.

Felt-tip Pen

These come in an almost endless selection of colors, and can be used to color in markings on petals.

Bleach

Color can be removed from paper with bleach. This is most often used to shade petals for a realistic appearance, such as for the Wild Rose on page 00. Bleach can be applied with a brush or poured into a small bowl for dipping. Lay the petals out on white paper to dry.

Inks

Colored inks in spray bottles can be used to shade petals. Make sure to allow the ink to dry completely before assembling flowers.

Gouache Paints

These can be brushed onto petals for shading. Alternatively, acrylic paints can be used. Make sure to allow the paint to dry completely before assembling flowers.

Varnish Spray

Paper flowers are long lasting but they can fade or droop over time. Coating them with matte spray will strengthen the petals and help them hold up longer.

Slotted Quilling Tool

This is the only tool required for quilling. It has a handle with a metal stick inserted in one end. The metal stick has a small cut (slot) where you can hook the quilling paper. For a beginner, this tool is a must have.

Pretty Imposters

Some paper flowers look so real, observers must walk up close and touch them to know they are handmade. With their vibrant colors, delicate textures, and distinctive shapes, these everlasting versions are just as elegant and alluring as natural flowers. They are especially appealing for weddings and other celebrations—paper flowers can be made long before the event, transport easy, and double as long-lasting mementos. Create gorgeous arrangements by combining two or more varieties, then decorate your home or give them as thoughtful gifts.

Calla Lily

1. Cut a piece of doublette crepe paper in half and place the half sheets one on top of the other. Using the template (page 142), cut out a pair of petals.

2. Glue the two layers together.

3. Make a ball out of air-drying clay. Form the ball into a 3" (7.6 cm) cylinder for the stamen, and roll the stamen over a cheese grater to give it texture.

4. Apply glue onto the end of the 18-gauge wire and gently push ½" (1.3 cm) into the center of one end of the stamen. Set aside to dry.

5. Place the center onto the calla lily shape.

6. Apply glue on the bottom right edge of the petal. Fold the bottom left edge over the wire and stamen, then fold the right edge over and adhere.

7. Wrap the wire with floral tape, beginning at the bottom of the petal.

MATERIALS

* doublette crepe paper, orange or ivory
* scissors
* craft glue
* air-drying clay, yellow
* cheese grater
* stem wire, 18 gauge
* florist tape

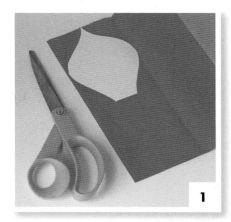

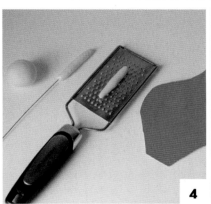

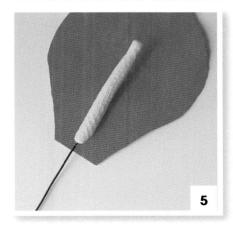

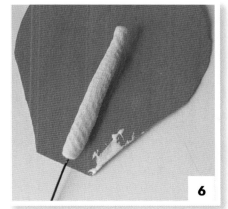

Narcissus

1. Using the templates (page 143), cut out three of the single petals and one of the joined petals from the white crepe paper.

2. Fold over four double-sided stamens and bind with florist wire. Secure the stamens to one end of a stem wire using florist tape; wrap the entire stem with tape. Cut a 1½" x 2¼" (3.8 x 5.7 cm) strip of yellow crepe paper; then fold it in half and pinch the folded ends. Wrap the stamens as shown and bind with wire. Glue the ends together.

3. Place the three joined petals in a triangle shape at the base of the flower center and bind with wire.

4. Place the next three petals alternating with the first three, as shown, and bind. Tug the petals gently so they flare out to shape the flower.

5. Wrap a stem wire with florist tape. Cut a 7" x 6" (17.8 x 15.2 cm) rectangle of dark green crepe paper, and apply glue to one side. Place the taped stem wire on one half of the rectangle and fold over to adhere.

6. Trim the outer edges into a long spear shape.

MATERIALS

* doublette crepe paper, yellow, white, and dark green
* florist wire, 26 gauge
* stem wires
* stamens
* florist tape
* scissors
* craft glue

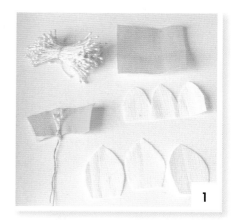

1

2a

2b

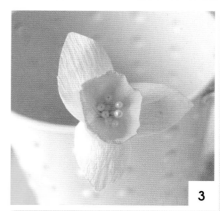

3

4

5

6

Daffodil

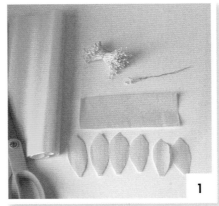

1

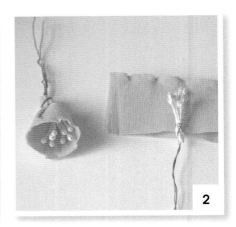

2

3

MATERIALS

* doublette crepe paper,
  yellow and orange
* florist wire, 26 gauge
* stem wires
* stamens
* scissors
* craft glue
* florist tape

INSTRUCTIONS

1. Cut six petals out of the yellow crepe paper using the template (page 142).

2. Fold over four double-sided stamens and bind with florist wire. Cut a 2¾" x 2½" (7 x 6.4 cm) strip of orange crepe paper, with the grain running breadthwise, and fold into half; then pinch the folded ends. Wrap the stamens as shown and bind with wire. Glue the ends together.

3. Place three petals in a triangle shape and bind with wire. Place the next three petals between the first three and bind.

4. Tug the petals gently so they flare out to shape the flower. Tape the stem with florist tape.

5. Make leaves as for Narcissus on page 17, steps 5 and 6.

Daisy

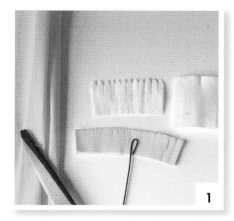

INSTRUCTIONS

1. Using the template (page 142), cut out the petals from the white crepe paper. Cut a 4½" x 3" (11.4 x 7.6 cm) strip from yellow crepe paper for the stamens. Form a loop in the end of a stem wire.

2. Fold the stamen piece in half along the stretch, and fringe the folded edge using scissors. Roll the stamen around the stem wire loop, and bind with wire.

3. Place the petals around the center and bind with wire.

4. Tug the petals gently so they flare out. Tape the stem with florist tape.

5. Cut out leaves from the dark green crepe paper, using the template (page 156). Wrap stem wires with florist tape, and glue the wires to the leaf backs. Wrap leaves together with the flower stems, using florist tape.

MATERIALS

* ✱ doublette crepe paper, yellow and orange
* ✱ florist wire, 26 gauge
* ✱ stem wires
* ✱ florist tape
* ✱ scissors

Tulip

1. Glue two layers of yellow doublette crepe paper together to form a long strip. Cut six petals out of the yellow crepe paper using the template (page 142).

2. Using the template (page 142), cut a strip of green paper and fringe the taller part into three; wrap around the stem wire, and glue in place to form the center.

3. Cut a 1½" x 2" (3.8 x 5.1 cm) rectangle from the black crepe paper and fringe one long edge into six pieces. Twist each fringe between your fingers.

3. Wrap the black stamens onto the center and bind with wire. Fold the ends of the black stamens back at 90 degrees.

4. Cup the petals by gently tugging from the center out in both directions.

5. Place three petals around the center, overlapping them as shown. Bind them to the stem with wire.

6. Place the next three petals alternating with the first three, and bind with wire

7. Tug the petals gently so they flare out and form a flower. Tape the stem with florist tape.

* doublette crepe paper, yellow
* crepe paper, black and green
* craft glue
* florist wire, 26 gauge
* stem wire
* florist tape
* scissors

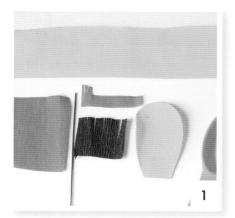

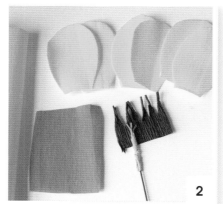

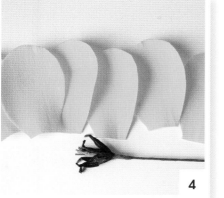

Stephanotis

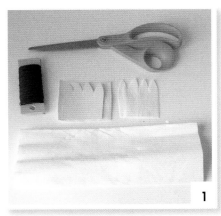

1

1. Using the template (page 143), cut out the petal strip from the white crepe paper.

2. Roll the strip, keeping the petals opposite each other on four sides; bind the lower edge with florist wire.

3. Tug the petals gently so they flare out to form a flower. Dip the end of a pearl pin in glue and push into center. Wrap the bottom of the flower and the wire with florist tape.

4. Repeat steps 1 to 3 to make several flowers; join them in a cluster by twisting their wire ends together. Wrap all together with florist tape.

2

MATERIALS

* **doublette or florist crepe paper, white**
* **florist wire, 26 gauge**
* **pearl pins**
* **florist tape**
* **scissors**
* **craft glue**

Sunflower

lengthwise. Layer the green and black strips and roll, dabbing glue to hold in place. Repeat with a black strip, wrapping this strip outside of the rolled black and green strips to form a large rolled center.

3. Cut two 3" (7.6 cm) circles from the thick catalog paper. Poke the stem wire into the center of one circle. Lay flat on circle and sandwich with second circle. Allow to dry.

4. Glue the rolled crepe paper center on top to complete the flower center.

5. Glue eight of the petals onto the center; then glue the remaining eight petals behind these to form an outer ring.

6. Cut a green scalloped circle and glue to the back, covering the catalog paper circles. Wrap the stem wire with florist tape, catching in a wired leaf as you wrap.

MATERIALS

* doublette or florist crepe paper, black and green
* crepe paper folds, yellow
* thick catalog paper
* craft glue
* scissors
* stem wire
* florist tape
* wired leaf

INSTRUCTIONS

1. Cut sixteen petals out of the yellow crepe paper folds, using the template (page 143). Cup the middle of the petals.

2. Cut one 2½" x 9" (6.4 x 22.9 cm) strip from both the black and green crepe paper. Fold the strips in half

Chrysanthemum

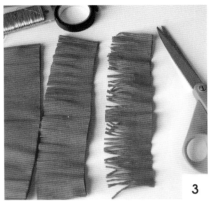

3

4

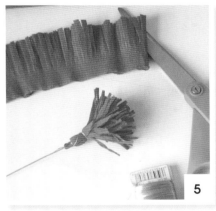

5

7

MATERIALS

* crepe paper folds, red, yellow, orange, and green
* stem wire
* florist wire
* florist tape
* scissors

INSTRUCTIONS

1. Cut several 2¼" (5.7 cm) strips across the crepe paper fold breadthwise.

2. Unfold the long strips. If using single-ply crepe paper, layer two strips; if using doublette, use one strip at a time.

3. Use scissors to make fringe halfway into one side of each strip. Twist the fringe between your fingers to shape it.

4. Bend a hook into the end of a stem wire. Hook it over the end of a fringed strip.

5. Roll the strip around the stem wire; bind the bottom with florist wire.

6. Continue to add strips, rolling and slightly pleating each strip to complete the flower. Bind with florist wire.

7. Add sepals (page 28) and wrap the stem with florist tape.

Forget-Me-Not

INSTRUCTIONS

1. Using five-petal flower punch, punch out desired number of flowers from the purple and pink crepe paper.

2. Using a pointed toothpick or wire, poke a hole in the center of each flower. Cut a stamen in half; poke the stamen wire through the hole and then glue the stamen head to the flower. Allow to dry.

3. Bunch the flowers and twist the stamen wires together. Add a stem wire and wrap with florist tape.

MATERIALS

* doublette or florist crepe paper, purple and pink
* paper punch of a five-petal flower
* stamens
* pointed toothpick or wire
* glue
* stem wire
* florist tape
* scissors

Iris

1. Cut out six 2½" x 4" (6.4 x 10 cm) rectangles from the crepe paper, using darker tones for three and lighter tones for three.

2. Using the template (page 144), cut the rectangles into six petals. Use the smaller template to cut three petels for the center.

3. Cut white florist wire into six 6" (16.2 cm) pieces. Apply glue to florist wire and adhere a wire to the back of each petal.

4. Cup the three center petals. Wrap them together and bind with tape onto stem wire.

5. Cup all six petals by bending the wire. Gently tug the petal edges to make them frill. Attach the three lighter toned petals, with wire sides inward, to form a closed bud.

6. Add the three darker toned petals, with wired sides outward, facing down, alternating the top three petals to finish the flower. Add more stem wire and tape to make the stem long and strong. Make leaves following the instructions in Narcissus (page 16) but using longer strips.

MATERIALS

* florist crepe paper, shaded, or any colors of doublette paper
* doublette crepe paper, green
* florist wire, 26 gauge
* white florist wire
* florist tape
* stem wire
* scissors

1

2

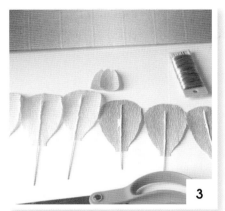

3

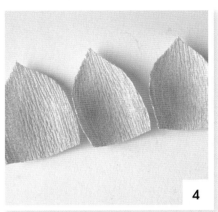

4

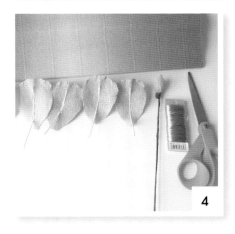

4

5

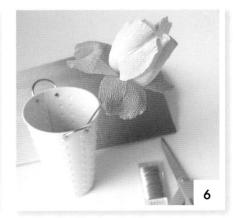

6

Winding Rose

1. Cut three 10" x 2¼" (25.4 x 5.7 cm) strips and two 10" x 1¾" (25.4 x 4.5 cm) strips from the purple paper.

2. Fold each strip into 1¾" (4.5 cm) equal parts and taper the tops into a petal shape. Unfold.

3. Cup each petal, and use a stem wire to roll back the upper edges of each petal.

4. Bend a loop in the end of a stem wire. Roll a narrow strip around the loop and tie the bottom with floral wire. Keep adding strips, narrow ones first, rolling and slightly pleating each strip to complete flower. Continue to bind with floral wire.

5. To create sepals, cut a wide strip from the green crepe paper and cut pointed fringes.

6. Wrap the sepals around the base of the rose. Wrap the base with florist tape and continue down the entire stem.

MATERIALS

* doublette crepe paper folds, purple
* crepe paper, green
* florist wire
* scissors
* stem wire

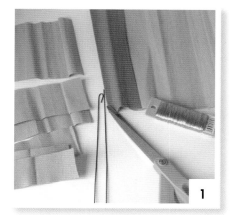

1

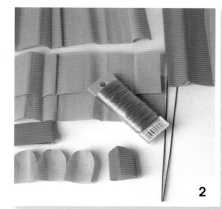

2

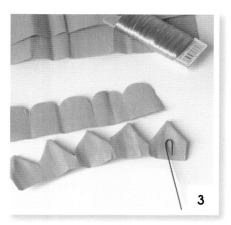

3

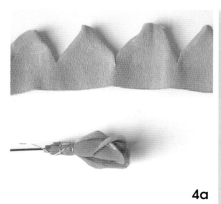

4a

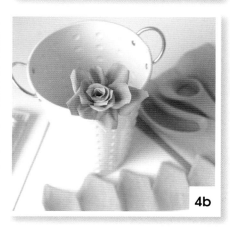

4b

4c

5

6

Country Rose

1. Using the template (page 144), cut fifteen petals out of the peach paper. Cup ten petals, with the darker tone inside.

2. Curl one side of the edges of two petals inward, with the darker toned side on top. Bend a loop in the end of the stem wire, and roll the two petals around the loop, overlapping them. Bind the bottom with florist wire, keeping the stem wire inside to make the rose center.

3. Curl both sides of the remaining petals outward, with the darker toned side up. Add two petals opposite each other and bind with stem wire.

4. Add more petals, binding with wire or dabbing glue to the petals overlapping each other.

5. Cup the remaining five petals in the opposite way, keeping the darker tone outside.

6. Apply glue and add the petals as the last layer of the rose. Add sepals and finish the stem following steps 5 and 6 in Winding Rose (page 28).

MATERIALS

* doublette crepe paper folds, peach
* crepe paper, green
* florist wire
* scissors
* stem wire
* craft glue

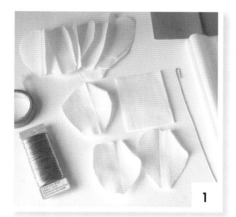

1

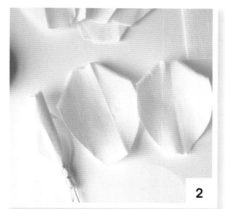

2

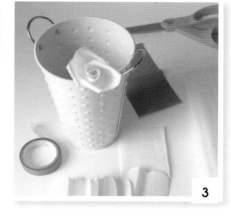

3

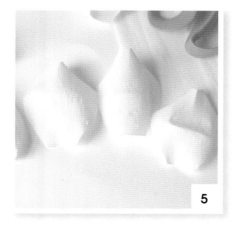

5

6

Rosebud

1

3

INSTRUCTIONS

1. Using the template (page 143), cut out six petals from the pink crepe paper. Cup petals, with the darker tone inside.

2. Curl one side of the edges of one petal so the darker tone is inside. Roll the other side of the petal vertically and bind with florist wire. Wind onto the stem wire to form the flower center.

3. Curl both sides of the remaining petals outward, with the darker toned side up. Overlap three petals around the center and bind with florist wire.

4. Add three more petals, binding with wire or dabbing glue to the petals, alternating placement of each petal.

5. Add sepals and stem following steps 5 and 6 for Winding Rose (page 28).

MATERIALS

* doublette crepe paper folds, double colored pink
* crepe paper, green
* florist wire
* scissors
* stem wire
* craft glue

Blooming Rose

INSTRUCTIONS

1. Follow steps 1 through 4 of the Rosebud instructions (opposite) to create a bud.

2. Add five more petals in another layer, binding with wire or dabbing glue to the petals overlapping one another. Add eight more petals to form the next layer to finish the flower.

3. Add sepals and stem following steps 5 and 6 for Winding Rose (page 28).

MATERIALS

* doublette crepe paper folds, double colored pink
* crepe paper, green
* florist wire
* scissors
* stem wire
* craft glue

Lilac

MATERIALS

* doublette crepe paper folds, purple
* florist wire
* scissors
* stem wire
* stamens
* florist tape
* craft glue

INSTRUCTIONS

1. Cut 1½", 2", and 2½" (3.8, 5.1, and 6.4 cm) squares from the purple crepe paper.

2. Fold each square into a triangle diagonally and then fold again to form a smaller triangle.

3. Taper the triangles into petal shapes. Unfold.

4. Using a pointed stem wire, poke a hole in the center of a petal. Cut a stamen in half and insert the wire through the hole. Glue stamen head to flower center. Allow to dry.

5. Wrap two or three stamens together with floral tape to make buds to start each bunch. Add flowers, wrapping with floral tape as you go, starting with smaller flowers on top and the larger flowers on the bottom.

3b

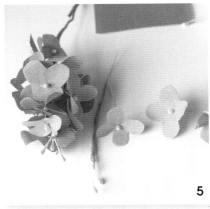

5

Cherry Blossom

MATERIALS

* doublette or florist crepe paper, pink
* stamens, yellow-tipped
* stem wire
* florist wire, 26 gauge
* florist tape
* scissors

INSTRUCTIONS

1. Using the template (page 151), cut out five petals from the pink crepe paper.

2. Fold and bunch three double-tipped stamens and bind with florist wire.

3. Form the flower following steps 3 and 4 in Violets (page 38).

Anemone

1. Cut a 2½" (6.4 cm) strip from a black crepe paper fold and open it. Cut a square out from the strip. Cut 1" (2.5 cm) strips from the paper napkins. Bend a loop in the end of the stem wire.

2. Wind napkin strips around the loop to make a round ball; bind with florist wire. Wrap the ball with the black paper square and bind again with wire.

3. Fold the rest of the black strip of crepe paper in half and fringe the paper along the fold, halfway to the opposite edge. Roll the fringe between your fingers to make them thinner.

4. Wrap the fringe around the black ball to form the center of the flower.

5. Using the templates (page 144), cut out five small petals and seven large petals from the white paper. Cup all petals and pinch the center top to make a swirl.

6. Apply glue to the bottom of five small petals and adhere to the flower center to form the inner ring.

7. Apply glue to the bottom of seven large petals and adhere to form the outer ring. Finish by taping with florist tape from the base of the flower down the length of the stem.

MATERIALS

* doublette crepe paper folds, white
* crepe paper folds, black
* paper napkins
* craft glue
* scissors
* stem wire
* florist tape

1

2

3

4a

4b

5

6

7

Violet

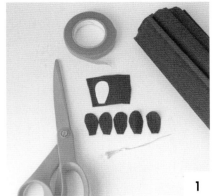
1

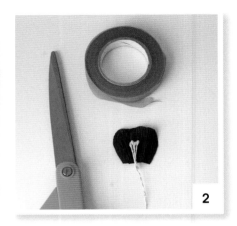
2

MATERIALS

* doublette or florist crepe
  paper, purple
* florist wire, 26 gauge
* stamens
* florist tape
* scissors

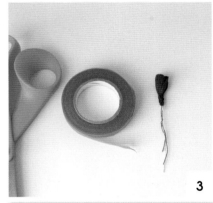
3

INSTRUCTIONS

1. Using the template (page 146), cut out five petals from the purple crepe paper.

2. Fold over two double-sided stamens and bind with florist wire.

3. Arrange the five petals around the stamens so they overlap each other. Wrap and bind with florist wire.

4. Tug the petals gently so they flare out to form a flower. Wrap the stem with florist tape. Repeat to create enough flowers to form a boutonniere.

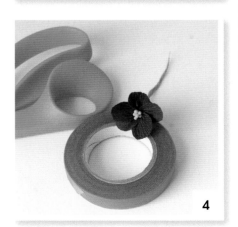
4

Statice

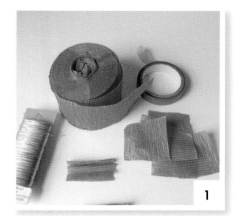

1

3

4

INSTRUCTIONS

1. Cut sixteen squares out of the streamer paper, ranging in size from 1½" to 2" (3.8 to 5.1 cm).

2. Accordion-fold the squares.

3. Fold the folded squares in half and bind with florist wire and tape.

4. Wind green florist tape onto a piece of stem wire. Then, starting with one flower on top, add three sets of two flowers and then three sets of three flowers in rows to form a statice bunch, taping each flower to the stem. Continue adding flowers until you reach the desired size.

MATERIALS

* **crepe paper streamer, purple or color of choice**
* **florist wire**
* **florist tape**
* **scissors**
* **stem wire**

Peony

1. Using the templates (pages 144 and 145), cut out twenty small petals and five large petals from the pale pink paper. Cup all the petals and pinch the top edges to frill slightly. Cut out a 3" (7.6 cm) square from the pale pink paper and set aside for the flower center.

2. Bend a loop in the end of a stem wire and make a ball out of tissue paper or paper napkin bits. Fold the square paper into a triangle and place the ball and stem wire loop inside the triangle.

3. Fold the top two corners over the ball to the center to make a bud shape, keeping the stem wire inside. Bind with florist wire.

4. Place three of the small petals around the bud, overlapping each other, and wrap with florist wire to form the center.

5. Add more petals, binding with wire or dabbing glue to the petals overlapping each other.

6. Cup the five large petals and glue around the flower to form outer petals. Add sepals and wrap the stem following steps 5 and 6 in Winding Rose (page 28).

MATERIALS

* florist crepe paper folds, pale pink
* florist wire
* scissors
* stem wire
* paper bits
* craft glue

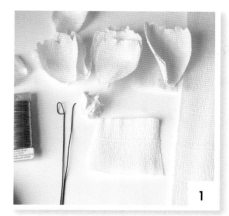

1

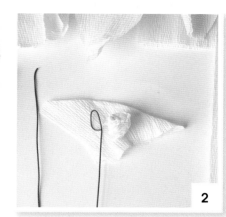

2

3

4a

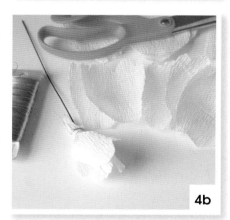

4b

5a

5b

6

Rosette

INSTRUCTIONS

1. Fold over three double-ended stamens and tie with florist wire. Using florist tape, tape the stamens to a piece of bent stem wire to form flower center.

2. Cut a 2¼" (5.7 cm) width strip from the crepe paper fold. Unfold the strip.

3. Fold over 1½" (3.8 cm) on one end of the strip and continue folding until the entire strip is folded. Cut the top of the folded rectangle into a gentle curve.

4. Open up the strip; then roll it around the stamens, gathering the bottom around the stem and allowing the edge to flare. Bind with florist wire as you wrap, continuing to the end of the strip.

5. Cut a 1½" x 3" (3.8 x 7.6 cm) strip from green crepe paper and fringe it, to make a sepal. Apply glue and adhere the sepal to the base of the rosette. Wrap the base of the sepal with florist tape and continue down the entire stem.

MATERIALS

* crepe paper folds or doublette, pink
* crepe paper, green
* stamens
* florist wire
* florist tape
* scissors
* stem wire

Lily of the Valley

1

3

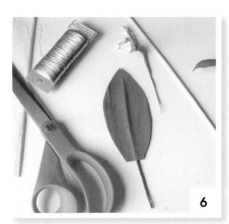

6

INSTRUCTIONS

1. Using the templates (page 145) and fine scissors, carefully cut out the flower shapes from the white crepe paper, making several in each size.

2. Roll each flower shape into a cylinder and glue the overlapping ends.

3. Cut a small double-end stamen in half, and insert one stamen into a cylinder. Gather the base around the stamen wire; tie with florist wire. Wrap the flower base and stamen wire with florist tape. Repeat for all the flowers. Cup the petals using the blunt end of a bamboo skewer.

4. Cut several large double-end stamens in half; wrap with florist wire and cover with florist tape.

5. To form a stem of flowers, start at the top with three large stamens one below the other. Add one small flower, two medium flowers, and two or three large flowers, wrapping with florist tape as you progress down the stem. Wrap in a stem wire to make stem longer and sturdier if needed.

6. Using template (page 145), cut out leaves. Glue two leaves together with a stem wire in between and allow to dry. Mark the veins with a skewer.

MATERIALS

* doublette crepe paper, white
* crepe paper, green
* florist wire, 26 gauge
* florist tape
* stamens, large and small
* fine scissors
* craft glue
* bamboo skewer

Carnation

4. Bend a loop into the end of a stem wire. Open up the strips; then roll a strip around the loop, gathering the bottom and allowing the frilly edge to flare. Bind with florist wire.

5. Continue rolling and frilling to form the flower center. Bind with florist wire after each strip is completely rolled.

6. Keep adding the strips until a full flower is formed.

7. Cut a 1½" x 3" (3.8 x 7.6 cm) strip from green crepe paper and fringe it to make a sepal.

8. Glue the sepal to the base of the carnation. Wrap the base of the sepal with florist tape and continue down the entire stem.

MATERIALS

* square paper napkins
* florist wire
* scissors
* stem wire
* craft glue

INSTRUCTIONS

1. Cut off the crimped edges of a paper napkin, and cut the center square into four equal strips.

2. Fold over 1½" (3.8 cm) on one end of a strip and continue folding until the entire strip is folded. Repeat for the other three strips. Cut the top of each folded rectangle into a gentle curve.

3. Cut tiny fringes into the top curved edges of the folded strips.

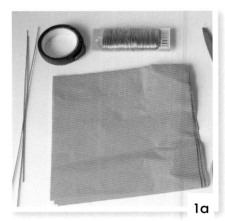

1a

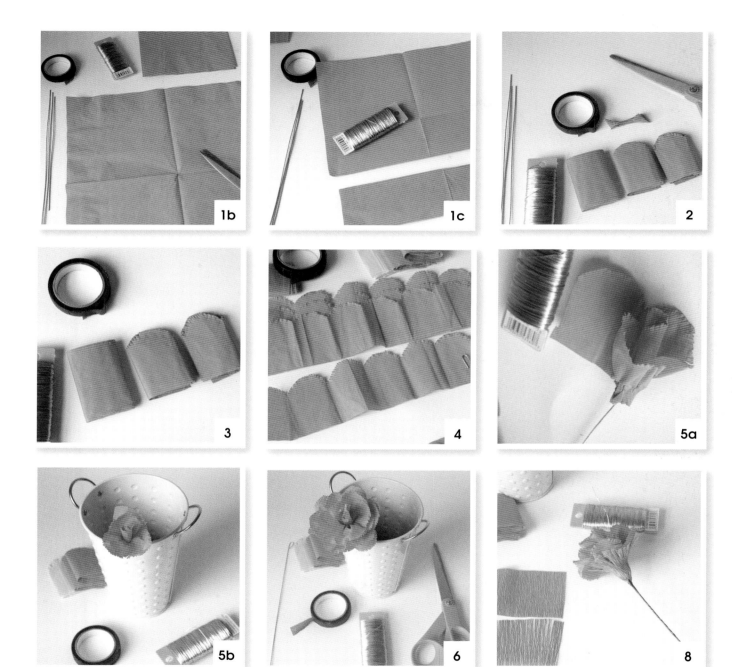

Dahlia

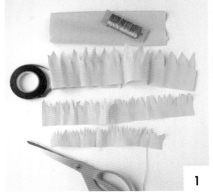

MATERIALS

* **doublette crepe paper folds, pink**
* **scissors**
* **stem wire**
* **florist wire**
* **craft glue**
* **florist tape**

INSTRUCTIONS

1. Cut two 20" x 2¼" (50.8 x 5.7 cm) strips, two 20" x 2¾" (50.8 x 7 cm) strips, and two 20" x 3" (50.8 x 7.6 cm) strips of the pink crepe paper.

2. Cut one long edge of each narrow strip into ¼" (6 mm) wide pointed fringes. Cut one edge of each medium strip into ½" (1.3 cm) wide pointed petal shapes, and finally cut each wide strip into 1" (2.5 cm) wide pointed petals.

3. Gently curl the fringed side of the narrow and wide strips with the blade of the scissors. Cup each petal of the largest strips and set aside.

4. Bend a loop in the end of a stem wire. Roll a narrow strip, curls inward, around the loop, and tie with florist wire to form the center. Repeat with the second narrow strip.

5. Repeat step 4 with the medium strips, this time keeping the curl outward. Dab with glue to secure.

6. Finish by adding the widest strips, cupping outward. Roll and dab with glue to secure.

7. Add sepals as for Winding Rose (page 28) and wrap the stem with florist tape.

Camellia

MATERIALS

* doublette crepe paper folds, pink or white
* doublette crepe paper folds, green
* florist wire
* stamens ,yellow tipped
* scissors
* stem wire
* craft glue

INSTRUCTIONS

1. Using the templates (page 146), cut out ten large petals and five small petals from the pink paper. Cup the petals and frill the edges. Fold and bind ten double-sided stamens with florist wire.

2. Overlap the five small petals and place the stamen in the middle. Then wrap and bind with florist wire to make the center.

3. Add five of the larger petals with cupped side outward for a second layer; bind with stem wire, dabbing glue to secure.

4. Add five more petals for a third layer, binding with wire or dabbing glue to the petals and staggering each petal. Lengthen stem by winding and taping to stem wire. Add sepals following instructions in Winding Rose (page 28).

Orange Blossom

1

1. Using the template (page 147), cut out five petal shapes from the white crepe paper.

2. Wind a 4" (10.2 cm) stem wire with a ½" (1.3 cm) wide strip of green crepe paper. Add the stamens around this to form the flower center.

3. Overlap the petals around the flower center. Wrap and bind with florist wire.

4. Curl all five petals using scissors to open out the flower. Cut out a leaf shape and wrap with florist tape to stem of flower. Group flowers together to form a bunch. Secure the bunch to stem wire by wrapping with florist tape.

MATERIALS

* **doublette or florist crepe paper, white**
* **doublette crepe paper, green**
* **stamens, orange tipped**
* **florist wire, 26 gauge**
* **stem wire**
* **florist tape**
* **scissors**

Orchid

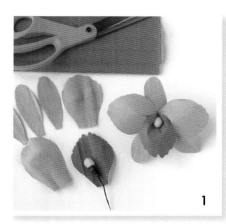

1

INSTRUCTIONS

1. Using the first template (page 147), cut out one center petal. Cut out two petals from the second template. Cut three of the tapered petals from the third template. Cup the side petals as shown and curl the tapered petals using scissors.

2. Make a ½" (1.3 cm) ball using the pale orange paper, referring to the Anemone center (page 36). Wrap the center petal around the ball, overlapping the lowers ends; bind with florist wire.

3. Place the side petals on opposite sides and bind with florist wire. Add the three tapered petals at the top and sides as shown. Create a leaf using the Lily of the Valley leaf template (page 145) and add to finish the flower.

MATERIALS

* doublette or florist crepe paper, purple
* doublette crepe paper, pale orange
* doublette crepe paper, green
* florist wire, 26 gauge
* florist tape
* scissors

Hyacinth

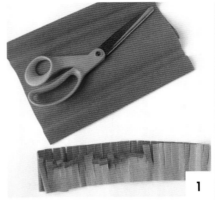

INSTRUCTIONS

1. Cut a 2¼" (5.7 cm) strip from a crepe paper fold as shown, keeping the grain vertical. Cut fringes at ¼" (6 mm) intervals.

2. Use the bamboo skewer to roll the fringes down, away from the darker color.

3. Dab glue to the strip and roll onto the stem wire, keeping the curl outward and making sure to wind several times at the top to form close petals at the top.

4. Glue down any loose ends to finish the flower. Wrap the remaining stem with a strip of green crepe paper.

5. Add leaves following steps 5 and 6 for the Narcissus on page 16.

MATERIALS

* doublette crepe paper, blue or purple
* crepe paper, green
* bamboo skewer
* stem wire, brown paper wrapped
* craft glue
* scissors

Crushed Rose

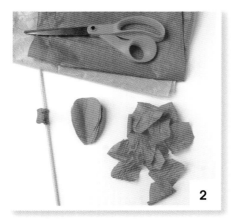

INSTRUCTIONS

1. Using the template (page 146), cut out the petals from the hot pink lokta paper.

2. Roll each petal on a bamboo skewer loosely breadthwise and push the ends toward the center to crush the petal. Carefully unravel petals and set aside.

3. Roll one petal and tie with florist wire to form the flower center. Wrap the center with three petals and bind with florist wire; then tie onto stem wire to form the stem.

4. Keep adding petals, dabbing with glue and tying with florist wire when necessary.

5. Add sepals following steps 5 and 6 of Winding Rose (page 28).

6. Cut out a leaf shape from the green paper and tape the leaf tip to the stem. Wind with green paper to finish stem.

MATERIALS

* handmade lokta paper or any similar lightweight paper, hot pink and green
* bamboo skewer
* craft glue
* scissors
* florist wire
* stem wire

Lily

MATERIALS

* florist crepe paper or doublette, yellow
* florist tape or crepe paper, brown
* crepe paper doublette, green
* marker, brown
* craft glue
* scissors
* stem wire
* florist wire

INSTRUCTIONS

1. Using the template (page 147), cut out six of the petals from the yellow crepe paper.

2. Using a brown marker, color dots on the six petals. Gently cup all petals.

3. Cut five 4" (10.2 cm) pieces of stem wire. Following the steps in Tulip (page 20), create green center.

4. Wind the pieces of stem wire with green paper. Tape the tips with the brown florist tape. Roll several times to form stamens. Gently bend the stamens at 90 degrees to form the stamen shape. Wrap the center and the stamens together with stem wire, using florist tape.

5. Add three petals in a triangle shape and bind with florist tape.

6. Repeat step 5 to add three more petals to form the flower.

Easter Lily

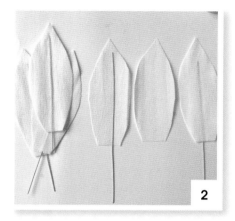

2

3

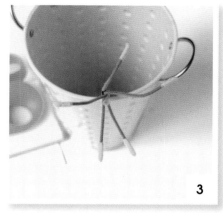

INSTRUCTIONS

1. Using the template (page 147), cut out twelve petals from the white crepe paper.

2. Wire the petals by sandwiching a stem wire between two petals and gluing them together.

3. Cut six 5" (12.7 cm) lengths of the green stem wire. Apply glue to a ½" (1.3 cm) orange strip of crepe paper and wind onto the tip of a green wire to form a pistil. Repeat with golden yellow strips of crepe paper to form five stamens. Bend stamens at 90 degrees. Bundle pistil and stamens and tape them together. Add stem wire and wrap together with florist tape.

4. Bend the six petals gently. Attach three petals in triangular shape to the center. Attach the other three alternating with the first three.

5. Cut four leaves, using the template on page 148. Make two leaves following instructions in step 2; attach them to the stem.

MATERIALS

* doublette crepe paper, white and green
* crepe paper folds, golden yellow and orange
* crepe paper, green
* florist wire, 26 gauge
* stem wire, green thread wrapped
* florist tape
* stem wire, 18 gauge
* scissors
* craft glue

Hibiscus

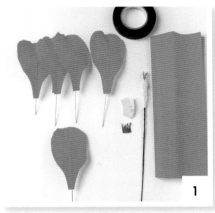

1

7

MATERIALS

* doublette crepe paper, orange, red, green, and yellow
* florist wire, 26 gauge
* florist tape
* stem wire, 18 gauge
* scissors
* craft glue

INSTRUCTIONS

1. Using the template (page 148), cut out ten petals from the orange crepe paper.

2. Wire the petals by sandwiching a stem wire between two petals and gluing them together as in the Easter Lily (page 53).

3. Cut a ¾" x 1" (1.9 x 2.5 cm) wide strip from the red crepe paper. Cut into four fringes and roll the tips. Fringe another ¾" (1.9 cm) wide strip of yellow crepe paper.

4. Apply glue to both of the strips and wind the red onto a stem wire at the tip. Wrap the yellow around the stem wire to make a center. Trim off excess.

5. Bend the five petals gently by bending the wire.

6. Attach the five petals to the center, taping them together with florist tape to form the flower.

7. Using the leaf template (page 148), cut two leaves; glue them together sandwiching a wire in the center. Trim the outer edges with pinking shears. Secure to stem.

Bird of Paradise

1

2

INSTRUCTIONS

1. Using the templates (page 149), cut out six petals for the flower: one yellow, two orange, and three in darker orange. Cut out one green pod and one blue anther from the third template.

2. Cup all petals, keeping the darker colors outside. Layer the petals in this order: green, yellow, orange, dark orange, making sure to keep the darker color facing down. Wind and tie with florist wire.

3. Add stem wire and tape with a ½" (1.3 cm) strip of green paper. Flare out the petals and glue the blue anther in between the orange petals.

MATERIALS

* **doublette crepe paper folds, yellow, orange, dark orange, blue, and green**
* **craft glue**
* **scissors**
* **stem wire**
* **florist wire**

Poppy

1. Using the template (page 150), cut out six petals for the flower from the orange crepe paper. Cut a thin strip from the golden yellow crepe paper and twist it to form a thread.

2. Cut a 4" (10.2 cm) square from a double layer of the green crepe paper. Pinch the center of the square and tie using florist wire. Crush a ball of green crepe paper.

3. Place a petal on a handkerchief, and fold over the handkerchief so the petal inside folds in half.

4. Place your palm on the covered petal, press down, and tug the hand-kerchief with your other hand to form crinkles on the petal. Cup the crinkled petals and set aside.

5. Tie 2 bundles of stamens with florist wire.

6. Place the crushed ball of crepe paper onto the pinched side of the green crepe paper and wrap the square around it to form a ball. Wind with florist wire. Wind the yellow thread onto the ball dividing the ball into half, then fourths, and then eighths. Tie with florist wire.

7. Add the stamens around the ball and spread them out to form the center. Wind again with florist wire.

8. Add three petals, dabbing glue, in a triangle form; add the next three petals, alternating them, to form the flower.

9. To make the bud, overlap three petals and roll; tie with florist wire. Add stem wire. Wind with a ½" (1.3 cm) green paper strip to finish the flower, winding several times to form a bump at the bud.

MATERIALS

* ✳ **doublette crepe paper folds, orange**
* ✳ **crepe paper, green and golden yellow**
* ✳ **florist wire**
* ✳ **craft glue**
* ✳ **scissors**
* ✳ **stem wire**
* ✳ **stamens, orange tipped**
* ✳ **an old handkerchief**

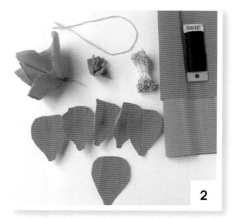

2

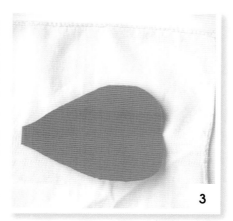

3

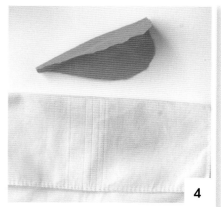

4

5

9

Wild Rose

1

1. Using the template (page 149), cut out the six petals from the pink crepe paper.

2. If a shaded color is desired, dip the bottom of each petal in a small, flat bleach-proof container of liquid bleach; allow to dry. When they are dry, cup the petals.

3. Make a ¼" (6 mm) ball out of ivory crepe paper, following step 2 for the Anemone center (page 36). Arrange yellow stamens around the ball. Wind and tie with florist wire.

4. Overlap the petals and wrap the center to form the flower. Tie with florist wire or glue in place. Add stem wire and wrap with florist tape. Tug the petals gently so they flare out to form a flower.

MATERIALS

* ✳ **doublette crepe paper folds, pink**
* ✳ **crepe paper, ivory**
* ✳ **crepe paper, green**
* ✳ **liquid bleach**
* ✳ **craft glue**
* ✳ **scissors**
* ✳ **florist wire**
* ✳ **stem wire**
* ✳ **florist tape**
* ✳ **stamens**

Sweet Pea

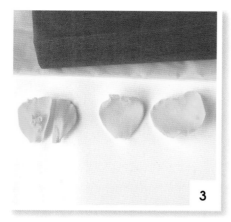

3

4

INSTRUCTIONS

1. Cut out two petals using the first sweet pea template (page 149) and one petal using the second template from the pink crepe paper. If you are using single crepe paper folds, use two layers for each petal.

2. Crush a small ball of the yellow crepe paper. Cup one of the small petals and place ball inside. Glue the petal in half to form the flower center. Cup the second small petal, wrap it around the center, and tie with florist wire.

3. Cup the large petal and wrap it around the others, keeping the cup outwards. Tie again with florist wire. Add stem wire if desired.

4. To add tendrils, wind a green paper strip onto stem wire and wind this onto a pencil. Remove and add to flower bunch.

MATERIALS

* crepe paper folds, pink or yellow
* crepe paper, green
* craft glue
* scissors
* florist wire
* stem wire

Dogwood

1

MATERIALS

* **doublette crepe paper folds, white**
* **crepe paper, green**
* **brown paint or marker**
* **craft glue**
* **scissors**
* **florist tape**
* **stem wire**

INSTRUCTIONS

1. Using the template (page 150), cut out four petals for the flower from the white crepe paper. Pinch the middle tip of each petal, and then cup all four petals.

2. Fringe a ¾" x 2" (1.9 x 5 cm) green crepe paper. Roll and tie with florist wire to form center.

3. Overlap the petals and wrap them around the center to form the flower. Tie with florist wire or glue in place. Add stem wire and wrap with florist tape. Flare out the petals and color in the pinched centers with brown paint or a marker.

4. Cut two leaf shapes for each leaf desired, using the template (page 150). Glue the layers together, sandwiching a length of florist wire down the center. Wind and tape onto the stem wire, arranging the flowers on opposite sides of the stem.

Anthurium

INSTRUCTIONS

1. Using the template (page 150), cut out the petal and cup the middle.

2. Follow steps 3 and 4 for Calla Lily to create the center (page 14).

3. Apply glue to the bottom of the petal, wrap the center with the petal, and tie with florist wire.

4. Shape the flower by reverse cupping the lower left and right corners and flaring out the flower.

5. Wrap the stem with florist tape.

MATERIALS

* **doublette crepe paper folds, red**
* **florist wire**
* **stem wire, 18 gauge**
* **air-drying clay, yellow**
* **cheese grater**
* **craft glue**
* **florist tape**

Pansy

1

1. Using the templates (page 150), cut out three of the small petals and two of the larger ones. Cup the petals.

2. Using gouache paints, shade the petals with black and blue. Allow to dry.

3. Wind a ¼" (6 mm) orange strip of crepe paper onto florist wire to form the stamen. Wind with stem wire for the center.

4. Place the colored petals in a triangle formation with the stamen in the center. Wind with florist wire. Glue the remaining petals to the back and tie to secure. Wrap the stem with florist tape.

5. Add a wired leaf and tape to the stem.

MATERIALS

* **doublette crepe paper folds in desired colors**
* **gouache paints, black and blue**
* **paintbrush**
* **florist wire**
* **scissors**
* **stem wire**
* **florist tape**

Gardenia

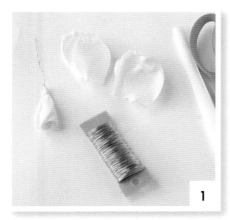

1

3

INSTRUCTIONS

1. Using the templates (page 151), cut out eleven large petals and three small petals from the white paper. Cup the eleven petals and pinch the top middle of the petals.

2. Overlap the three small petals and roll. Tie the roll with florist wire to form the flower center.

3. Add the five larger petals with cupped side outward around the center; bind with florist wire and dab with glue to secure in place.

4. Add six more petals in a staggered arrangement, again binding with wire or dabbing with glue to secure. Add stem by winding and taping to stem wire. Add sepals using instructions in Winding Rose (page 28).

MATERIALS

* **doublette crepe paper folds, white**
* **crepe paper, green**
* **florist wire**
* **scissors**
* **stem wire**
* **florist tape**
* **craft glue**

Jumbo Rose

1. Using the templates (pages 152 and 153), cut out fourteen small petals and fourteen large petals from the red crepe paper.

2. Cut an 8" (20.3 cm) square from red crepe paper. Create a red center by crushing a larger ball of paper; follow steps 2 and 3 in Peony (page 40).

3. Curl one side of a larger petal, keeping the lighter side up. Cup the petal with the lighter side up.

4. Apply glue to the inside and roll and wrap around the center, keeping the top closed.

5. Cup all petals, keeping the darker side on top. Curl both sides of all petals.

6. Apply glue to smaller petals and wrap the center with three petals.

7. Glue five of the smaller petals to the inner ring and the rest to the next rings to form the flower.

8. Finish the flower by adding the larger petals, overlapping each other and gluing in place to achieve desired size. Tie with florist wire and tape the stem.

9. Cut a 3" (7.6 cm) strip from the green crepe paper and cut sepals out of it. Glue onto the stem, and wrap the stem with florist tape. Using the template (page 151), cut two leaf shapes from the green crepe paper with pinking shears. Wire the leaves together and tape to the stem.

MATERIALS

✳ doublette crepe paper folds, red
✳ crepe paper folds, green
✳ craft glue
✳ scissors
✳ pinking shears
✳ stem wire
✳ florist wire
✳ florist tape

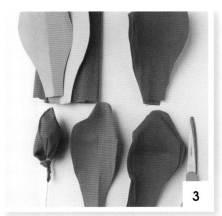

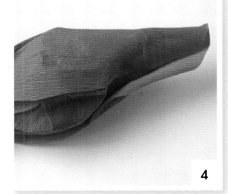

Forsythia

1

1. Using the template (page 151), cut out twelve flower shapes from the yellow crepe paper.

2. Roll the petals and bind the base with florist wire.

3. Curl the petals outward using scissors. Wrap flower base and the stem with brown florist tape.

4. To form the branches, wrap the stem wire with brown tape. Add flowers to stem wire, attaching a single one at the top and then adding flowers on alternating sides. Use twelve flowers for each bunch.

MATERIALS

* doublette or florist crepe paper, yellow
* florist wire, 26-gauge
* florist tape, brown
* stem wire
* scissors

Bells of Ireland

1

INSTRUCTIONS

1. Cut a 2" wide by 5" (5.1 x 12.7 cm) long strip from green crepe paper.

2. Fold the strip in half and pinch the folded edge to frill it.

3. Roll to make two layers and trim off excess. Wind the base with florist wire and florist tape. Flare out the bell by inserting your fingertips to form a bell shape.

4. Wrap a stem wire with florist tape. Add flowers to the stem, starting with one flower on top; keep adding flowers a set at a time: one set of two flowers, and then two sets of three flowers and a final set of four flowers to form a bunch.

MATERIALS

* **crepe paper folds in green**
* **florist wire**
* **scissors**
* **stem wire**

Ranunculus

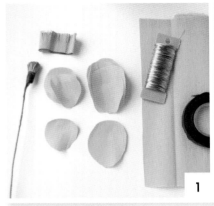
1

5

MATERIALS

* doublette crepe paper, peach
* scissors
* craft glue
* stem wire, 18 gauge
* florist tape
* florist wire

INSTRUCTIONS

1. Using the templates on page 154, cut out eight small petals, seven medium petals, and eight of the large petals from the peach paper. Cup the tops of the petals.

2. Fringe a 1" (2.5 cm) wide strip of green crepe paper. Wrap with stem wire and roll to form the flower center; tape in place.

3. Overlap three small petals and place the flower center in the middle. Wrap, and bind with florist wire to make a bud.

4. Add five of the small petals with cupped side inward and bind with stem wire, dabbing glue to secure. Add the seven medium petals in the next layer.

5. Add the eight large petals, staggering each petal and binding with wire or dabbing with glue. Add sepals following steps 7 and 8 in Carnation (page 44).

Magnolia

3

7

INSTRUCTIONS

1. Using the templates (page 157), cut out eight small and six large petals from the white crepe paper. Cup all petals and pinch the top to make a swirl.

2. Cut a 3" (7.6 cm) square from green crepe paper. Create a green center following steps 2 and 3 in Peony (page 40).

3. Cut a 2" (5.1 cm) strip from green and cut sepal patterns. Twist the pointed ends. Cut a similar strip from burgundy and curl using blade of scissors.

4. Apply glue to green strip and wind onto the cone-shaped center. At the bottom, glue two layers of the burgundy. Trim off excess.

5. Apply glue to the bottom of the petals and arrange five of the small petals in the inner ring and the six large petals in the outer ring to form the flower.

6. Cut out four leaf shapes using template (page 154). Glue two leaves together, sandwiching a wire down the center. Repeat for the other leaf. Wrap the leaf wire with florist tape; set aside.

7. Overlap the remaining three small petals and roll loosely to form a bud. Tie with florist wire. Glue the open top together to form a closed bud.

8. Add a stem wire to the bud, and wrap together with florist tape. Continue wrapping the stem, adding the flower and then the leaves as you wrap.

MATERIALS

* doublette crepe paper folds, white
* crepe paper folds, green and burgundy
* craft glue
* scissors
* stem wire
* florist tape

Playful Posies

Crafting paper flowers can be fun for the entire family; many of the flowers in this section are easy enough for children to make. Some styles are made with paper you may already have around the house, like recycled magazines and newspapers, cupcake liners, or paper napkins. To simplify the cutting part, some flowers are made from paper-punch shapes or die cuts. Traditional Mexican paper flowers, like the Flore de Papel, Papel Rose, Mexican Poppy, and Bonbon Flower create a fiesta mood with their brilliant colors and celebratory shapes.

Spiral Flower

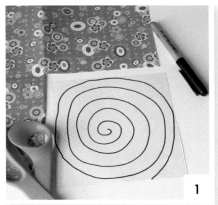
1

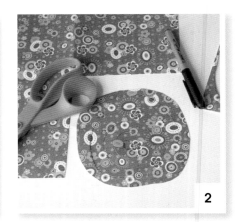
2

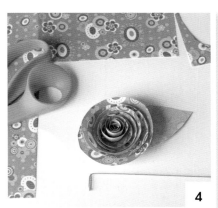
4

MATERIALS

* scrapbook paper, various colors
* craft glue
* scissors
* florist tape

INSTRUCTIONS

1. Cut a 12" x 12" (30.5 x 30.5 cm) piece of scrapbook paper into four equal squares. Draw a spiral onto the back side of one square.

2. Cut the spiral out.

3. Roll the spiral up tightly, starting from the outside and using the middle as a base; then allow the spiral to uncoil slightly. Apply glue to the base and press the spiral edge into the glue to secure.

4. Cut a leaf shape and glue the flower onto the leaf. Bend a loop in the end of a stem wire; then bend the loop at a 90 degree angle to the stem. Glue the loop to the base of the flower to form the stem. Apply florist tape to finish.

Spiral Fluted Flower

INSTRUCTIONS

1. Follow steps 1 and 2 for the spiral flower, opposite. Then recut the outer edge of the spiral using shaped-blade scissors or pinking scissors.

2. Finish the flower, omitting the stem. Glue the flowers and leaves onto a wreath base.

MATERIALS

* scrapbook paper, various colors
* craft glue
* shaped or pinking scissors
* wreath base

Daisy Wheel

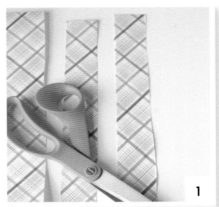

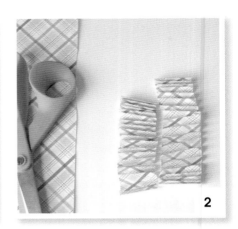

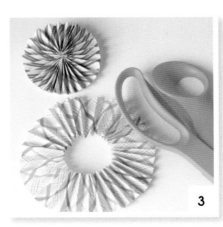

MATERIALS

* scrapbook paper, various colors, 12" x 12" (30.5 x 30.5 cm) (Using diagonal striped paper creates great spiraling effect)
* craft glue
* scissors
* wreath base

INSTRUCTIONS

1. From a piece of scrapbook paper, cut two 1½" (3.8 cm) strips for each flower.

2. Fold the 1½" (3.8 cm) strips into accordion folds.

3. Glue the end folds to each other to form a circle. Then glue the center together to close the shape.

4. Repeat using varying widths of paper strips to create different sizes of daisy wheels. Glue onto a wreath base, overlapping the wheels and mixing the sizes.

Pinwheel

2

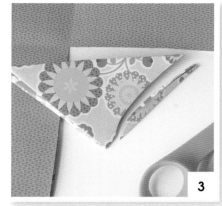

3

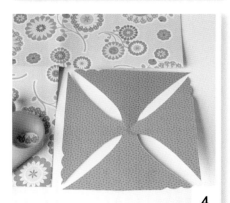

4

5

INSTRUCTIONS

1. Cut a 12" x 12" (30.5 x 30.5 cm) piece of scrapbook paper into four equal squares.

2. Fold one square into a triangle by folding along the diagonal. Fold the triangle in half again.

3. Cut off a small portion of the triangle on both folded sides, beginning a short distance from the center and tapering to the outer points.

4. Open the shape and, using shaped-blade scissors, taper the left point of each wing as shown.

5. Fold the pointed ends toward the center and adhere with craft glue or hot glue, overlapping the points to create a pinwheel shape. Punch out a shape of your choosing and glue onto the center of the flower. Apply glue to a skewer and attach to the back of the pinwheel flower.

MATERIALS

* double-sided scrapbook paper, various colors
* paper punch (small flower)
* craft glue or glue gun and glue sticks
* scissors
* shaped-blade scissors
* skewer

Flore de Papel

1. From the crepe paper, cut one yellow and seven hot pink 12" x 9" (30.5 x 22.9 cm) rectangles, keeping the grain along the 9" (22.9 cm) side.

2. Lay yellow crepe paper flat, place two bamboo skewers on opposite sides, and roll to the center evenly and tightly.

3. Place upright and slide paper down to form a crushed roll. Remove the skewers.

4. Apply glue on flat side and roll up to form a disc shape.

5. Repeat steps 2 and 3 with the seven hot pink rectangles to make the petals.

6. Apply glue on open ends and adhere to center.

7. Glue a skewer to the back.

8. Make variations of this flower by adding more rolls.

MATERIALS

* crepe paper folds, hot pink, yellow, whisper pink, green, and ivory
* bamboo skewers
* glue gun and glue sticks or craft glue
* scissors

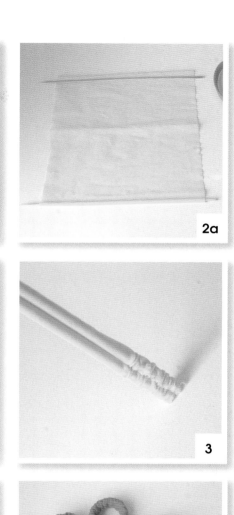

1

2a

2b

2c

3

5

6

7

Heart Punch Rose

MATERIALS

* construction paper, color of choice
* construction paper, green
* heart punch, medium and the next smaller size
* craft glue
* scissors

INSTRUCTIONS

1. Using both punches, punch out numerous heart shapes from the construction paper. Punch out three petals with the smaller punch for the flower center. Curl the larger hearts on both sides to make petals.

2. Cut a 2" (5.1 cm) circle out of the construction paper.

3. Apply glue to the tip of the hearts and adhere seven petals to the circle base, slightly overlapping petals to fill the round base.

4. Apply glue and add four petals to form a second layer, placing the petals opposite each other.

5. Glue three of the smaller heart punch-outs together so they overlap one another; then roll to form the center. Glue onto the flower. Cut out two leaves and glue to the bottom.

Heart Punch Camellia

MATERIALS

* construction paper, color of choice
* construction paper, green
* heart punch, medium
* craft glue
* scissors
* yellow crepe paper
* sunburst punch

INSTRUCTIONS

1. Punch out seven heart shapes from the construction paper. Curl the hearts on both sides to make petals.

2. Cut a 2" (5.1 cm) circle out of the construction paper. Punch out a green sunburst. Roll a 2" x 1" (5.1 x 2.5 cm) piece of yellow crepe paper into a small tube and cut into three small pieces to form stamens.

3. Apply glue to the tips of four petals and adhere them to the circle base, slightly overlapping and evenly spaced.

4. Apply glue to the tips of three petals and add them in a triangle to form a second layer.

5. Glue the sunburst to the center. Glue the three stamens to the center. Punch out a green heart to form a leaf and glue to the bottom.

1

4

Heart Punch Dahlia

MATERIALS

* * construction paper, yellow and orange or any color of choice
* * construction paper, green
* * heart punch, medium
* * craft glue
* * scissors

1

INSTRUCTIONS

1. Punch out thirteen heart shapes from the construction paper. Roll to form a cone shape, and glue the overlap.

2. Cut a square out of the construction paper for the flower base.

3. Apply glue to the tip of the cones and adhere seven petals to the base, making sure the petals fill the base and touch side to side.

4. Apply glue to tips and add five petals to form a second layer.

5. Cut two strips of orange and yellow paper; cut fringe halfway into the strips of paper and roll to form the flower center. Glue the fringed center in place. Cut out green leaves and glue to the bottom.

Music Note Flower

MATERIALS

* double-sided scrapbook paper, music notes prints (printing music sheets onto scrapbook paper would also work)
* scrap of paper from mailers or magazines.
* craft glue
* scissors
* pinking shears
* bamboo skewers
* rhinestone brooch or button

INSTRUCTIONS

1. Using the templates (page 155), cut out six large and five small petals from the music note sheets Cut out a 2¼" (5.7 cm) square for the base and a 3" (7.6 cm) circle for the center using pinking shears.

2. Curl both sides of all petals using bamboo skewers.

3. Cut a 1" (2.5 cm) wide black strip of paper from a glossy page of a magazine. Create a black Daisy Wheel following instructions for Daisy Wheels (page 74).

4. Cut ¼" (6 mm) fringes into the circle and curl with scissors.

5. Glue the large petals to the square base, arranging the petals so they overlap each other and form a circle. Layer the five smaller petals on top.

6. Add the fringed circle and then the black Daisy Wheel to form the center. Add a rhinestone brooch or button to the center to finish up.

1

Dahlia Pom

MATERIALS

* tissue paper, color of choice
* florist wire
* scissors

INSTRUCTIONS

1. Cut six 5" x 9" (12.7 x 22.9 cm) rectangles from the tissue paper and stack them.

2. Accordion-fold the sheets into ½" (1.3 cm) folds breadthwise and tie the center with florist wire.

3. Trim a long narrow triangle from each side of both ends.

4. Fan out the folds into a circle. Separate the tissue layers by gently pulling them apart to fluff into a ball as shown.

Tissue Peony

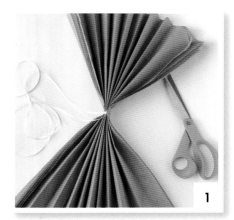

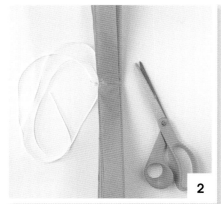

INSTRUCTIONS

1. Stack eight sheets of the tissue paper. Accordion-fold at 1" (2.5 cm) intervals. Tie a florist wire in the middle.

2. Round ends of both sides. Loop a thin ribbon at wire to hang.

3. Fan out the folds into a circle.

4. Gently pull the sheets apart, one by one, to fluff into a ball.

MATERIALS

* tissue paper, color of choice
* florist wire
* scissors
* ribbon

Papel Rose

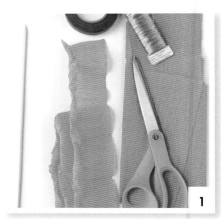

1

2

MATERIALS

* crepe paper folds in colors of choice
* bamboo skewers
* craft glue
* scissors

INSTRUCTIONS

1. Cut a 2½" (6.4 cm) strip from the fold breadthwise. Open the strip and curl the top edge of the strip using a bamboo skewer.

2. Dab glue to the strip and roll tightly to adhere to a bamboo skewer; this will form the flower's center. Continue rolling the flower, shaping the rolled edge to flare out and dabbing the lower edges with glue to hold in place.

Newsprint Dahlia

MATERIALS

* a paper flyer or newspaper ad
* craft glue
* scissors
* bamboo skewers
* shaped paper punch

INSTRUCTIONS

1. Tear out two sheets from the flyer. Accordion-fold the paper sheet widthwise and then fold in half.

2. Trim off the edges to form half of a petal shape, so that when opened, it forms a full petal.

3. Open out and glue open edges together to form a flower wheel shape.

4. Repeat steps 1 and 2 with a second piece of paper but trim off more paper to form a shorter wheel shape. Turn over shape and glue on top of the first. Punch out a small shape from the newsprint and glue to the center. Glue a bamboo skewer to the back to finish flower.

Cupcake-Liner Dahlia

MATERIALS

* * cupcake liners, large, white or pink
* * cupcake liners, large, green
* * bamboo skewers
* * craft glue
* * scissors
* * pinking shears

INSTRUCTIONS

1. Flatten three cupcake liners, fold them in half, and then refold again to make a quarter.

2. Cut ½"(1.3 cm) deep fringes on the cupcake liner quarter, following the creases on the liner, preferably centering a crease in each petal. Taper the fringes to form pointed petals.

3. Roll the petals to form the center, keeping the liner folded in quarters. Dab glue to keep in place. Trim off the bottom point.

4. Repeat steps 1 and 2 with three more liners to form the flower base and with a green liner to form the sepal. Unfold these pieces.

5. Layer and glue the three flower base pieces together, gluing only in the center. Glue the three rolled center pieces to the center of the flower base. Fluff out the petals to form a full flower.

6. Glue the bamboo skewer to the back of the flower and glue on the green sepal, creating a sandwich to form the back of the flower. Cut out a leaf shape from the green cupcake liner using pinking shears, and glue it to the skewer.

Cupcake-Liner Daffodil

MATERIALS

* * cupcake liners, large, yellow or color of choice
* * cupcake liner, small, patterned
* * construction paper, green
* * bamboo skewers
* * craft glue
* * scissors
* * buttons
* * florist wire

INSTRUCTIONS

1. Flatten two of the large cupcake liners, fold them in half, and then refold again into three equal portions. Taper the edges into pointed petals shapes.

2. Stack contrasting buttons, and thread them together using florist wire. Twist and tie at the back. Snip off excess.

3. Open out the larger liners to re-form cupcake liner shapes. Layer them, staggering the petals.

4. Glue the layers together. Add the smaller cupcake liner to form the cupped center.

5. Glue on the button center. Glue the flower to a bamboo skewer. Cut a construction paper leaf and glue it to the back of the flower.

Cupcake-Liner Poppy

1

1. Flatten three cupcake liners, fold them in half, and then refold again to make quarters.

2. Taper the quarters into rounded petal shapes.

3. Flatten a yellow cupcake liner and follow instructions in Spiral Flowers (page 72) to form a spiral flower center. Using pinking shears, cut a small circle from black crepe paper to fit the cupcake base.

4. Open up the three liners from step 2. Layer the three liners, alternating the petals, and glue them together.

5. Add the black circle and the yellow spiral center to form the flower.

6. Cut two leaf shapes from construction paper. Glue the bamboo skewer to the back of the flower. Add the leaves to sandwich the skewer to finish the back.

MATERIALS

* cupcake liners, red dotted or design of choice
* cupcake liner, yellow
* crepe paper, black
* construction paper, green
* bamboo skewers
* craft glue
* scissors
* pinking shears

Paper Napkin Daisy

MATERIALS

* printed paper napkins, green and pink or any contrasting prints of choice
* craft glue
* scissors
* florist wire
* bamboo skewers

INSTRUCTIONS

1. Cut each napkin in half. Layer all sheets and accordion-fold the stack breadthwise at 1" (2.5 cm) intervals.

2. Separate the sheets and refold all separately as single sheets. Using scissors, round both ends of the green napkin. Trim off 2" (5.1 cm) from the pink napkin, and round the edges.

3. Cut out a 3" (7.6 cm) wide strip from the pink napkin and fold lengthwise at 2" (5.1 cm) intervals. Cut slits in both folded edges. Roll and tie the center with florist wire.

4. Refold the accordion folds, layering the pink napkin on top and following the accordion fold markings.

5. Tie the center to the bundle. Fan out and glue open ends together. Fluff out the center. Glue a bamboo skewer to the back to finish the flower.

3

4

Upcycled Map Wall Flower

1. Cut out fifteen 8" (20.3 cm) squares from an old atlas or map. Trim the edges, if desired. Glue adjoining sides together to form cones. Cut a 5" (12.7 cm) round base from thick cover of a magazine or catalogue.

2. Glue the cones to the round base, keeping the tips straight so the cones form a circle.

3. Cut a 4" (10.2 cm) strip of the pink crepe paper fold breadthwise. Open the strip refold at 2½" (6.4 cm) intervals; round off the top to form rounded petal strips.

4. Using the templates (page 155), cut out six large petals and five smaller petals from the cardstock. Curl the edges of the petals using a bamboo skewer.

5. Glue the large cardstock petals, in a circle to the center of the flower. Repeat with the small petals. Allow to dry.

6. Dab glue onto the bottom of the pink petal strips and gently tuck the strips behind the large cardstock petals to form two layers.

7. Create a Daisy Wheel (page 74) and add to the center. Add a brooch or button to finish the flower. Add a small ribbon loop on the back for hanging, or use pushpin to hang.

MATERIALS

- ✳ old atlas or map
- ✳ magazine or catalog
- ✳ scrapbook paper
- ✳ craft glue
- ✳ scissors
- ✳ crepe paper folds, whisper pink
- ✳ cardstock, music note or pattern of choice
- ✳ bamboo skewer
- ✳ brooch or button
- ✳ piece of ribbon or pushpin

1

2

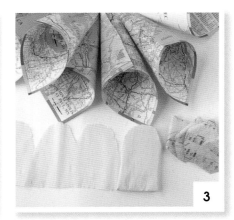

3

5

6

Bridal Hair Flower

INSTRUCTIONS

1. Using the templates (page 156), cut out seven of the large and eleven of the small petals from the white crepe paper. Cut out a 3" (7.6 cm) square for the base.

2. Cup all petals and frill them.

3. Glue the large petals to the base as shown, overlapping the petals to create a round base.

4. Repeat step 3 with six of the small petals, creating the next layer inside.

5. Repeat step 3 with five of the small petals to form the last layer. Add a brooch or button to finish the flower. Turn it into a hair flower by hot gluing a metal clip or U-pin to the back.

MATERIALS

* **doublette crepe paper, white**
* **heirloom brooch or button**
* **craft glue**
* **scissors**

 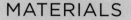

Mexican Poppy

1

2

3

INSTRUCTIONS

1. Stack three sheets of dark green and eight sheets of red. Trim three sheets of yellow and three sheets of light green tissue paper, as shown, and center them over the yellow.

2. Accordion-fold all sheets together, forming strong crease lines. Separate the color sets and refold along crease lines. Round the ends of the red tissue set. Trim the dark green and light green sets to pointed shapes to form the sepals and center, respectively. Cut ½" (1.3 cm) wide slits onto the yellow set.

3. Layer all the sets back together again in the same order, carefully sliding in all the layers following the accordion folds. Tie center with florist wire. Loop a ribbon in for hanging.

4. Gently pull the sheets apart, one by one to fluff into a flower.

MATERIALS

* **tissue paper, dark green, light green, yellow, and red, or color of choice**

* **florist wire**

* **scissors**

Recycled Sunflower

2

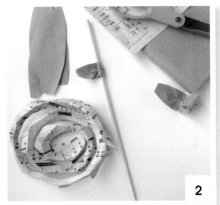

4

6

MATERIALS

* double-sided scrapbook paper, music notes prints or music sheets
* scrap of paper from mailers or magazines
* brown paper bag
* bamboo skewer
* craft glue
* scissors

INSTRUCTIONS

1. Using the templates (pages 156 and 157), cut out the seven petals and two leaves from the brown bag. Curl and crush the petals and leaves on a bamboo skewer following step 2 in Crushed Rose (page 95).

2. Draw and cut out spiral flower shape from a 6" (15.2 cm) square of the music note paper. Crease and fold in half along the spiral. Follow step 3 in Spiral Flower to create flowers (page 72).

3. Cut a 3" (7.6 cm) square from the music note sheet.

4. Glue the curled brown paper petals onto the base, curling inward.

5. Glue on the spiral flower to form the flower center.

6. Glue bamboo skewer to the back. Add two curled petals to stem to form leaves.

TIP: You can do this with newspaper or colored paper too.

Upcycled Flower

INSTRUCTIONS

1. Cut out two 4½" (11.4 cm) squares from the catalog, choosing images that you like. Cut one more square from a contrasting color. Cut out one leaf shape, fold in half, and then accordian fold diagonally to make veins. Unfold.

2. Fold the square into triangles, folding diagonally; repeat again three times to create a small triangular wedge. Round off the open end with scissors.

3. Repeat step 2 with the remaining two paper squares. Each time round off the ends a bit closer to the center; this will create smaller scalloped circles when opened.

4. Tear a page from the catalog and roll corner to corner, dabbing glue to form a stem.

5. Fringe a strip of paper at ½" (1.3 cm) intervals, dab glue, and roll to form the flower center.

6. Cut off two scalloped petals from the smaller circle. Overlap the open ends and glue to form a cone.

7. Layer the two scalloped circles and glue together. Glue the cone on top. Add the center. Add the leaf to the back and then glue to the stem. Allow to dry.

MATERIALS

* old catalogs with glossy paper
* craft glue
* scissors

Bonbon Flower

1. Cut a 4" x 6½" (10.2 x 16.5 cm) strip from a crepe paper fold, keeping the grain vertical.

2. Bring the lower corner up and fold into a triangle. Bring the top corner down and fold into a smaller triangle. Pinch the pointed tip and twist gently. Twist the tail to form a cup-shaped petal. Form five petals for a flower.

3. To form the flower center, follow step 1 and 2 of Amemone (page 36), Using crepe paper in any color desired.

4. Add the petals to the center and tie with florist wire. Trim off length of petal twists if needed. Add stem wire if desired.

MATERIALS

* crepe paper folds, pink, orange, and yellow, or any color of choice
* florist wire
* stem wire
* scissors

1

Bonbon Dahlia

INSTRUCTIONS

1. Create six petals following the instructions for the Bonbon Flower.

2. Make a green center, following step 3, opposite.

3. Fringe a 3" (7.6 cm) double layered strip of goldenrod crepe paper and wrap the ball center to form stamens.

4. Add the six petals to the center, keeping the open side upwards and tie with florist wire. Trim off length of petal twists if needed. Add stem wire and tape the stem.

TIP: Try variations by adding more layers of petals.

MATERIALS

* doublette crepe paper, yellow, white, and dark green
* florist wire, 26 gauge
* stem wires
* florist tape
* scissors

Fire Flowers

1

4

MATERIALS

* construction paper, red, purple, and violet or color of choice
* die cuts, optional
* crepe paper folds, golden yellow
* craft glue
* scissors
* wire cutter
* bamboo skewers

INSTRUCTIONS

1. Using the template (page 157) cut out eleven petals from the construction paper. If using die cuts or the template for the Fantasy Flower (page 158), use two six-petal die cuts and cut apart into eleven petals.

2. Cut a 4" (10.2 cm) wide strip from the crepe paper fold. Fringe a double layered strip. Dab glue onto the paper and roll onto the bamboo skewer to form the flower center.

3. Fold all petals in half.

4. Glue petals to the bamboo skewer with the center overlapping from alternate sides.

5. Glue all petals on to create the desired flower length. Cut off the remaining portion of visible bamboo skewer using wire cutter. Apply glue to a new bamboo skewer and insert into the bottom of the flower to form tall stem. Allow to dry.

7. Arrange in tall vases.

TIP: Try using patterned thick scrapbook paper to create modernistic flowers.

Fantasy Flower

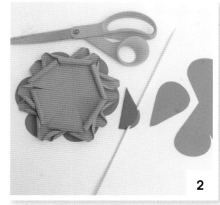

INSTRUCTIONS

1. Use two die cuts or cut out petals using the template (page 158) and curl both sides of all petals. Extend the petals of the third die cut inward by cutting toward the center. Curl and roll all six petals fully inward.

2. Use a green die cut as the flower base, and layer the two curled die cuts on top, staggering the petals. Place the third smaller one on top. Add buttons to form the flower center.

3. Apply glue to all layers and sandwich the bamboo skewer between the green and pink layer.

4. Cut off one petal from the green die cut. Fold the petal in half and glue to the bamboo skewer to form a leaf. Allow to dry.

TIP: Use patterned scrapbook paper to vary the look.

MATERIALS

* six-petal die cuts, hot pink and green or color of choice or template and construction paper
* craft glue
* scissors
* bamboo skewers
* buttons

Playful Peony

1

1. Using two die cuts, or the template for Fantasy Flowers (page 158), cut out petals from the red and purple construction paper. Curl and roll all petals inward using bamboo skewers.

2. Extend the petals of the third die cut inward by cutting toward the center. Curl and roll all six petals fully inward.

3. Cut a circle from the yellow die cut and fringe the circle, making small ¼" (6 mm) slits. Curl the fringe using the blade of the scissors.

4. Use a yellow die cut as the flower base, and layer a red and purple die cut on top, aligning the petals. Place the third, smallest die cut on top.

5. Apply glue to all layers and sandwich the bamboo skewer between the yellow and purple layer.

6. Add the fringed yellow circle and the button to make center.

7. Cut off one green petal from the green die cut. Fold the petal in half and glue to the bamboo skewer to form a leaf. Add another leaf on the opposite side. Allow to dry.

TIP: Try making these flowers in patterned cardstock.

MATERIALS

* six-petal die cuts, green, yellow, purple, red, or color of choice, or use template and construction paper or cardstock
* craft glue
* scissors
* bamboo skewers
* buttons

Cardstock Lily

INSTRUCTIONS

1. Using the template (page 158), cut out twenty-five petals from the cardstock. Cut a 2½" (6.4 m) square to form the flower base.

2. Curl eleven petals, using the blade of scissors. Bend the tips of the remaining petals in half, creating 1" (2.5 cm) crease lines on all petals.

3. Glue the flat petals on the base, overlapping them and creating a circle base.

4. Glue the curled petals in the next layer.

5. Cut a 3" (7.6 cm) wide strip from a different color of cardstock and fringe the strip at ¼" (6 mm) intervals. Curl the fringe using scissors and roll to form centers.

6. Glue the center to the flower.

MATERIALS

* **cardstock, colors of choice**
* **craft glue**
* **scissors**

Newsprint Poppy

3

4

MATERIALS

* a paper flyer or newspaper
* construction paper, black
* bamboo skewers
* florist wire
* florist tape, brown
* craft glue
* scissors

INSTRUCTIONS

1. Cut out six 8" (20.3 cm) squares from the newsprint.

2. Fold the squares in half diagonally, then unfold. Fold in the corners to meet at the center, then refold in half.

3. Fold the shape in half in the opposite direction.

4. Use bamboo skewers to curl the square corners.

5. Twist the triangular bottom to form cupped petals.

6. Cut a 6" (15.2 cm) square from newsprint. Crush and make a 2" (5.1 cm) ball. Wrap ball to form center, following instructions for Anemone center (page 36).

7. Fringe a strip of black paper. Curl the strip with blade of scissors. Wrap the center with fringe, and glue in place or tie with stem wire.

8. Apply glue to the bottom of the petals and adhere three petals to the center, arranging the petals in triangular shape. Tie with florist wire.

9. Add the next three petals, alternating the first three. Cut a leaf shape from black paper and glue to the bottom of the flower.

10. Wrap the stem with brown florist tape.

Fiesta Flower

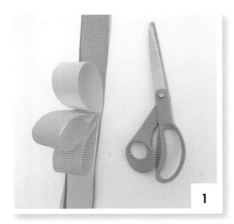

1

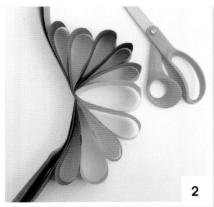

2

INSTRUCTIONS

1. Cut twelve 18" x 2" (45.7 x 5.1 cm) strips from construction paper. Stack them together and staple them at the center.

2. Roll the ends into the center and glue in place, working in order until you form a circle.

3. Cut two concentric circles using pinking shears. Glue them to the flower center.

MATERIALS

* **construction paper in any colors of choice**
* **tacky glue**
* **scissors**

Streamer Rose

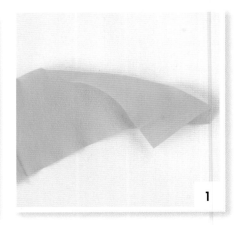

MATERIALS

* crepe paper streamer or folds, whisper pink or color of choice
* bamboo skewers
* florist wire
* florist tape
* craft glue
* scissors

INSTRUCTIONS

1. Use a streamer or cut a 2½" (6.4 cm) strip from the fold breadthwise. Open the strip a fold the top corner down to form an elongated triangle.

2. Dab glue to the strip and roll tightly to the middle of the triangle to form the flower center.

3. Refold the strip to create an overlapping triangle. Roll the center to the end of the triangle.

4. Repeat step 3 until flower is desired size. Trim the strip and glue to the bottom. Bind the flower with florist wire, and wire to a bamboo skewer. Finish stem with florist tape.

Bowtie Fleur

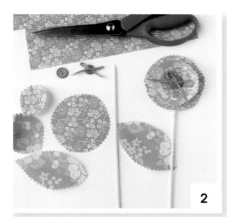

2

INSTRUCTIONS

1. Cut out three concentric circles from the scrapbook paper using pinking shears. Use ribbon spools or bottle caps as guides.

2. Make a cut from the edge to the center on each of the smaller two circles. Overlap the cut edges and glue to form cone shapes.

3. Thread a ribbon through a button and tie a bow.

4. Layer all the circles and glue in place. Glue the button in the center.

5. Cut a leaf shape from the scrapbook paper. Glue the leaf and flower to a bamboo skewer.

MATERIALS

* scrapbook paper
* ribbon spools or bottle caps
* craft glue
* scissors
* pinking shears
* bamboo skewers
* ribbon
* button

Protea

1. Remove the hardbound cover of the book. Take four sheets at once and fold the top right corner down to create a diagonal crease line. Unfold the triangle.

2. Fold the leftover bottom rectangle up, tearing the joint to where the crease line of the rectangle ends.

3. Refold the top right corner down (see to step 1) to create a perfect folded triangle.

4. Fold the triangle in half by bringing the bottom right tip to meet the top of the book.

5. Repeat the above steps to create more flaps with four pages at a time. Finish all the pages to form a full protea flower.

6. Form a stem by attaching a bamboo skewer or stick with glue or wire.

MATERIALS

* old books
* craft glue
* scissors
* bamboo skewers or stick
* stem wire

Origami Blossoms

Origami, the Japanese art of paper folding, is the method used for making the flowers in this section. The goal of this art is to transform a flat sheet of paper into a finished sculpture through folding and sculpting techniques. Technically, because some of the flowers in this section incorporate cuts or glue, they are not considered to be true origami. However, a dab of glue here and there will allow you to attach stems or stamens to your flowers, so go ahead and get creative. Think beyond paper; why not fold square napkins into camellias for your next dinner party?

Tulip

1. Cut scrapbook paper into an exact 6" x 6" (15.2 x 15.2 cm) square.

2. Fold square in half, lengthwise and breadthwise, unfolding after each fold.

3. Make diagonal folds and unfold.

4. Fold side triangle inward to make the "water bomb base," where one triangle sits on another.

5. Fold both bottom corners to top.

6. Turn over, and repeat step 5 to create a square shape.

7. Flip the flap over so no slits are visible. Repeat on the other side.

8. Fold to center again to form pockets on both sides.

(continued)

MATERIALS

* lightweight scrapbook paper
* craft glue
* glue gun and glue sticks
* scissors

1

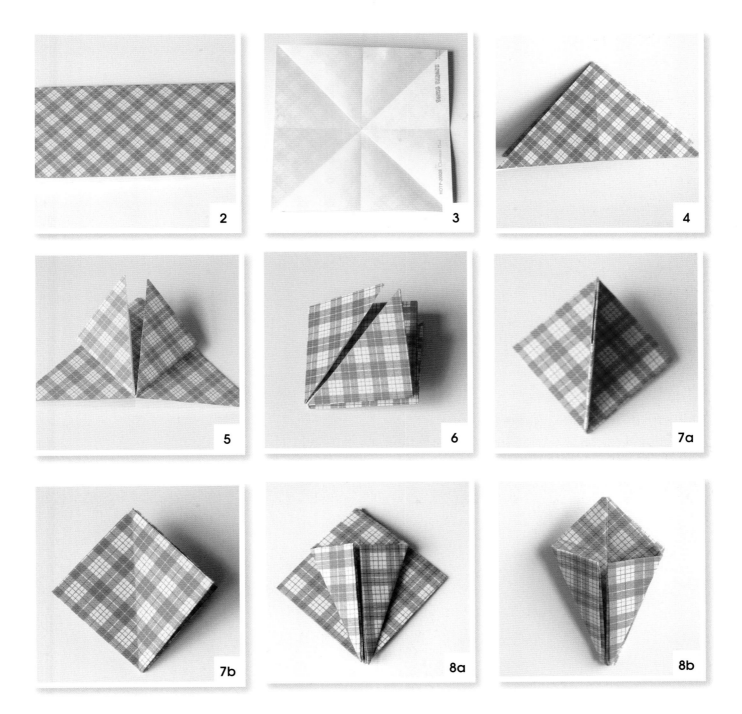

9. Dab glue in pockets and insert one tip into pocket to secure.

10. Repeat step 9 on the other side.

11. Pull pocket sideways to expand fully.

12. Press the base down on table to form square base.

13. Peel four petals.

14. For the stem, cut scrapbook paper into 8" x 8" (20.3 x 20.3 cm) square.

15. Fold diagonally and unfold.

16. Fold top corners to the center, forming a kite shape.

17. Fold bottom sides to the center.

18. Fold the sides again to meet the center.

19. Flip over and fold in half.

20. Fold over in half once more.

21. Peel leaf to form stem and leaf.

22. Dab glue onto the stem and poke the stem onto the small hole in the bottom of the flower.

23. Arrange in a metal planter. Use glue gun to adhere stem to pot.

9

10

11

12a

12b

13

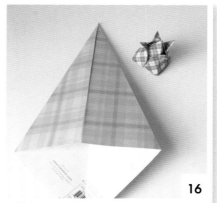

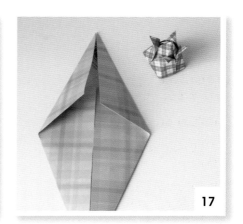

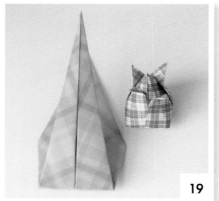

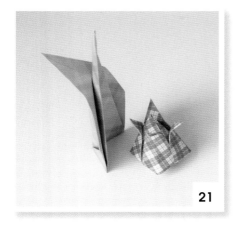

Origami Circle Flower

5. Fold the top left edge in to align to the center, forming an upside down kite shape.

6. Turn it over (side to side) and fold the bottom up in a triangle shape.

7. Turn over again and fold in half vertically.

8. Repeat steps 2 to 7 to make thirteen shapes per flower. Open out the back pocket of the lower triangle.

9. Dab glue in pocket and insert the front of another triangle.

10. Repeat step 9 with all the pieces, finally inserting the front of the first triangle into the pocket of the last to form a circle.

11. Dab glue onto a pointed tip of bamboo skewer and insert one tip into triangle to secure.

MATERIALS

* lightweight scrapbook paper or newspaper
* craft glue
* scissors
* bamboo skewers

INSTRUCTIONS

1. Cut scrapbook paper into thirteen exact 4" x 4" (10.2 x 10.2 cm) squares. Cut one out and keep that as a template for cutting the rest.

2. Fold diagonally, then unfold. Repeat for opposite diagonal.

3. Fold four corners inward to meet at the center.

4. Turn the square on point. Fold the top right edge in to align to the center.

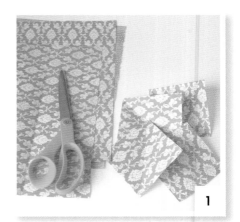

1

Kusudama Flower

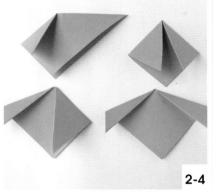

2-4

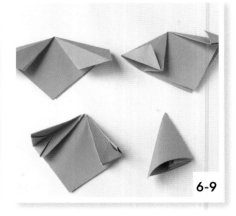

6-9

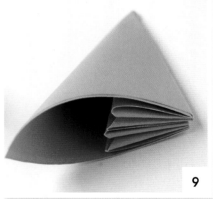

9

MATERIALS

* scrapbook paper
* craft glue
* scissors
* stem wire, brown paper wrapped, or bamboo skewers

INSTRUCTIONS

1. Cut scrapbook paper into exact 6" x 6" (15.2 x 15.2 cm) squares.

2. Make diagonal fold to form exact triangle.

3. Fold two opposite corners down to meet bottom corner at center and form a square. Crease well.

4. Open the left flap and refold, folding the flap in half.

5. Repeat step 4 with the opposite side flap, creasing well.

6. Open out the left flap and fold over, using crease line to make kite-shaped flap. Repeat with right flap.

7. Fold both tips upward (shown on the top right.)

8. Fold the flap over in half using crease lines. Repeat on right side.

9. Fold over to get shape shown.

10. Make six units out of paper and join them at the center to form flower. Set aside to dry.

11. Glue to stem wire or bamboo skewers.

Origami Sunburst

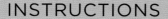

2-6

INSTRUCTIONS

1. Cut a 6" x 6" (15.2 x 15.2 cm) square from cardstock.

2. Fold in half and unfold to create crease. Fold both sides inward to meet at center and form a rectangle.

3. Fold all four corners inward to meet at center.

4. Fold the two sides inward to meet at center.

5. Fold in half lengthwise.

6. Fold strip into two to form double-petal shape, and fan out petals.

7. Repeat above steps with three more squares, creating three more sets of petals.

8. Attach all four petal sets at the middle with glue. Glue bamboo skewer to the back to form flower.

MATERIALS

* cardstock, color of choice
* craft glue
* scissors
* skewers

Origami Lily

3. Fold two opposite corners inward to meet at center and form a square base.

4. Keeping open end upward, fold the sides inward to meet at the center.

5. Turn it over and repeat step 4 to form a kite shape.

6. Open the left flap out and flip over to right to create a triangle shape from the flap.

7. Repeat above step with the right flap. Turn it over and repeat with the other two flaps.

8. Fold the bottom tip at half point to create a crease line. Open out.

9. Fold in the left and right top sides to meet at the center.

10. Turn it over and repeat step 9.

11. Open out flap and press down to form a pointed flap that faces down.

12. Fold flap up using crease line.

13. Turn it over and repeat step 12 to result in last shape shown.

14. Use a bamboo skewer to roll the four petals.

15. Apply glue to blunt end of bamboo skewer and poke through center to adhere.

MATERIALS

* **lightweight scrapbook paper**
* **craft glue**
* **scissors**
* **bamboo skewers**

INSTRUCTIONS

1. Cut scrapbook paper into exact 6" x 6" (15.2 x 15.2 cm) squares.

2. Make diagonal folds and unfold in both directions. Fold in half lengthwise and breadthwise, then unfold.

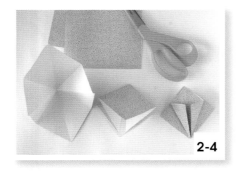

2-4

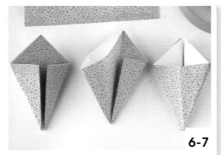

6-7

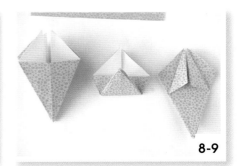

8-9

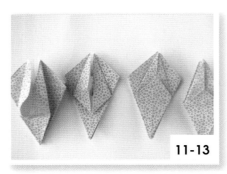

11-13

14

15

Origami Buttonhole

MATERIALS

* scrapbook paper, color of choice
* craft glue
* scissors
* pinking shears

2-5

INSTRUCTIONS

1. Cut a 6" x 6" (15.2 x 15.2 cm) square from scrapbook paper. Use smaller squares for smaller flowers.

2. Make diagonal folds and unfold; fold lengthwise and breadthwise, keeping the colored side up.

3. Bring opposite ends together to form square base, like Origami Lily (page 118), with colored side inside.

4. Fold the left and right side to the center to form second shape, keeping open ends down.

5. Turn over and repeat step 4.

6. Open out flower. Use pinking shears to curve the petals.

7. Create Origami Tulip leaf (page 112) using 6" (15.2 cm) paper, following steps 14–21

8. Glue flower stem to leaf and sandwich flower with leaf stem.

Origami Rose

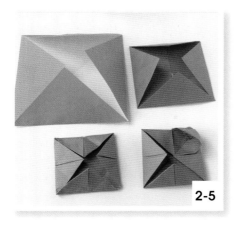

2-5

MATERIALS

* origami paper, 8" (20.3 cm) square, peach, or any lightweight paper cut into 8" (20.3 cm) squares
* origami paper, green
* craft glue
* bamboo skewer
* scissors

INSTRUCTIONS

1. Using a piece of 8" x 8" (20.3 x 20.3 cm) origami paper, fold the paper lengthwise and breadthwise to create creases. Unfold.

2. Fold four corners inward to meet at center, forming a square.

3. Repeat step 2, folding corners inward to meet at center.

4. Turn it over and repeat step 3 to create bottom left shape.

5. Lift the flap below each corner. Gently but firmly push the corners down and pull up flap to form bottom right shape.

6. Repeat above step with the remaining three flaps. Curl the four petals with a bamboo skewer.

7. Lift the remaining four flaps from the back up and curl with bamboo skewer.

8. Use a 4" (10.2 cm) square paper and repeat the above steps to create a smaller flower. Glue the flower into the center of larger flower.

9. Roll an 8" (20.3 cm) square of green paper corner to corner to form a stem. Dab glue to adhere the ends. Create leaf following Tulip leaf instructions (page 112). Cut off half and glue to stem. Glue stem to Rose.

Origami Camellia

MATERIALS

* printed paper napkins or newsprint
* any paper, yellow or contrasting color
* craft glue
* scissors

INSTRUCTIONS

1. Trim paper napkin to 8" (20.3 cm) square. Create a petal base following instructions from Origami Rose (page 121, steps 1 to 8).

2. Cut a 3" x 1" (7.6 x 2.5 cm) strips of yellow paper. Fringe one edge. Roll to create a center stamen. Glue center to petal base.

Origami Forget-Me-Not

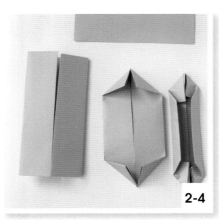

2-4

5-6

MATERIALS

* cardstock, blue and yellow
* craft glue
* scissors
* bamboo skewers

INSTRUCTIONS

1. Cut a 6" x 6" (15.2 x 15.2 cm) square from cardstock.

2. Fold in half and unfold to create crease. Fold both sides inward to meet at center to form a rectangle.

3. Fold all four corners inward to meet at center.

4. Fold the two sides inward to meet at center.

5. Turn over and fold in half lengthwise.

6. Fold strip into two to form double-petal shape.

7. Repeat above steps with three more squares, creating three more sets of petals.

8. Fringe a strip of yellow paper. Curl fringe with scissors. Apply glue and roll to form the flower center.

9. Glue all four petal sets together with the yellow stamen in the middle. Glue bamboo skewer to the back to form flower.

Quilled Florals

Thin paper strips are curled, coiled, and shaped in the delicate art of paper quilling, also called filigree. The paper is wound around a quill and glued to create a basic coil shape. These shaped coils are then arranged to form flowers, leaves, and various ornamental patterns similar to ironwork. You can purchase the paper already cut into thin strips, so the fun part begins right away. Some of the flowers in this section are created in many parts with traditional quilling techniques, using a quilling tool and then gluing the parts in place to make a greeting card or small framed artwork. Others, like the dandelion and jumbo fringed flower, use quilling methods on a larger scale to create great décor accents.

Quilled Forget-Me-Not

HAPPY

BIRTHDAY

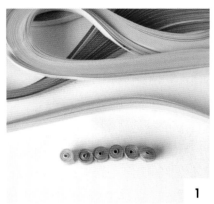

1

4

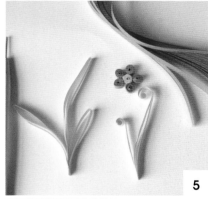

5

MATERIALS

* quilling paper, ¼" (6 mm), hot pink, yellow, and green
* craft glue
* scissors
* quilling tool

INSTRUCTIONS

1. Cut five 12" (30.5 cm) strips from the hot pink quilling paper. Slip the end of the strip into the slotted needle and roll. Glue the end to the roll. Repeat for others.

2. Pinch the rolls to form oval petals.

3. Cut one yellow 12" (30.5 cm) from the yellow quilling paper. Roll using quilling tool to form center; glue end to roll.

4. Glue the petals to the yellow center.

5. Cut green strips and form long loops for leaves. Curl the ends of some strips to form stems. Glue onto card.

Quilled Box Topper Flower

INSTRUCTIONS

1. Cut six 17" (43.2 cm) strips from the hot pink quilling paper. Slip the end of the strip into the slotted needle and roll. Place down and allow to uncoil. Glue the end to the roll with a dab of glue. Repeat for the other five petals.

2. Pinch opposite sides of the rolls to form petals.

3. Cut one yellow 8" (20.3 cm) strip from the yellow quilling paper. Roll, using quilling tool to form center.

4. Glue the petals together at their bases forming a circle. Glue the yellow center on top.

5. Cut leaf shapes from the crepe paper and arrange on the box top. Glue the flowers over the leaves.

MATERIALS

* **quilling paper, ¼" (6 mm), hot pink and yellow**
* **crepe paper**
* **craft glue**
* **scissors**
* **quilling tool**

Quilled Daffodil

MATERIALS

* quilling paper, ¼" (6 mm), yellow, orange, and green
* craft glue
* scissors
* quilling tool
* cardstock

INSTRUCTIONS

1. Cut six 17" (43.2 cm) strips from the yellow quilling paper. Follow steps 1–2 in Box Topper Flower (page 127) to make petals.

2. Glue a yellow and an orange strip together, end to end. Roll using quilling tool, starting from yellow to form a large roll. Glue the end to the roll. Press the center gently down to form double-shaded cup center.

3. Cut one yellow and one orange paper strip into ⅛" (3 mm) thin strips, 1½" (3.8 cm) long. Cut the yellow into three ½" (1.3 cm) strips. Roll the orange strip twice around the end of a yellow strip; cut, and glue in place to form a stamen. Repeat for the other two stamens.

4. Apply glue to one end of the petals and glue to cardstock base to form flower shape.

5. Glue the center on top, where the petals meet.

6. Glue the three stamens inside the cupped center to form flower.

7. Add the green strips to form stem and outlines of leaves.

Quilled Hydrangea

3

1. Cut four 17" (43.2 cm) strips from the purple quilling paper. Slip the end of the strip into the slotted needle and roll. Place down and allow to uncoil as shown in Box Topper Flower (page 127). Glue the end to the roll.

2. Pinch one end of each roll to form petals.

3. Cut one 6" (15.2 cm) strip from the yellow quilling paper. Roll using quilling tool to form center. Glue end in place.

4. Apply glue to rounded side of the petal and adhere to the yellow center. Repeat with the other three petals.

5. Create fifteen flowers in different shades of purple.

6. Make green leaves following the petal instructions above, but pinch both ends to form elongated leaves. Glue two shapes together to form a leaf.

7. Curl one end of several 5" (12.7 cm) green strips to form stems.

8. Glue the flowers to a cardstock paper. Layer them create a three-dimensional effect. Add leaves and stems.

MATERIALS

* quilling paper, ¼" (6 mm), different shades of purple
* quilling paper, ¼" (6 mm), yellow and green
* cardstock
* craft glue
* scissors
* quilling tool

Jumbo Fringed Flower

1. Cut two long 9" (22.9 cm) wide strips from a piece of 18" x 24" (45.7 x 61 cm) magenta construction paper. Fold in half and cut fringes three-fourths of the way into the folded side.

2. Open out and fold again, making the bottom edges ½" (1.3 cm) apart. Secure with clip if necessary. Glue together.

3. Apply glue and roll to form flower.

4. Repeat using the remaining strip to finish flowers, dabbing glue as you go along to secure.

5. Cut a green strip and fold every 2" (5.1 cm). Trim sides to form sepal shape. Glue sepals to flower. Apply glue to the thick stem wire and adhere to bottom of the flower. Set aside to dry.

6. Cut leaves out of green construction paper. Fold in half and then fold diagonally to form veins. Apply glue to stem wire and adhere it to the back of the leaf. Wind leaves, stem, and flower stem together with florist tape.

7. Arrange in tall vases.

MATERIALS

* construction paper, magenta, lavender, and green
* stem wire, brown paper wrapped
* craft glue
* scissors
* glue gun and glue sticks, optional
* florist tape

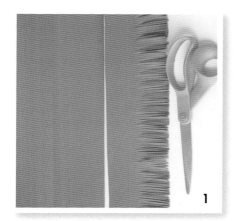

1

2a

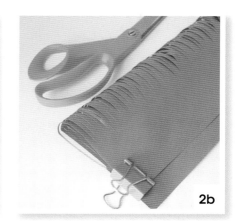

2b

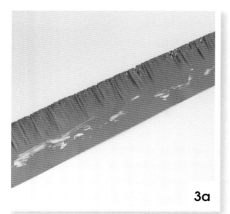

3a

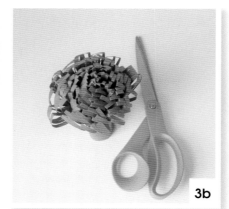

3b

4

5a

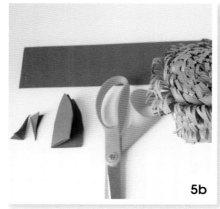

5b

6a

Quilled Bouquet

MATERIALS

* quilling paper, ¼" (6 mm): blue and yellow for wild flower, red and yellow for marquise flower, red and black for poppy, green for leaves
* quilling paper, ⅛" (3 mm): two-tone pink and green for foxglove
* quilling tool
* craft glue
* scissors
* white card stock

BLUE WILD FLOWER

1. Cut five 12" (30.5 cm) strips from the blue quilling paper. Slip the end of a strip into the slotted needle and roll. Allow the roll to uncoil slightly. Adhere the end to the roll with a tiny dab of glue.

2. Pinch the bottom and indent the top of the roll to form a heart shaped petal. Repeat for all the petals.

3. Cut one 8" (20.3 cm) strip from the yellow quilling paper. Roll using quilling tool to form center. Adhere the end to the roll with a tiny dab of glue.

4. Apply glue to the petals and adhere to the yellow center.

MARQUISE FLOWER

1. Cut five 17" (43.2 cm) strips from the red quilling paper. Slip the end of a strip into the slotted needle and roll. Place down and allow to uncoil. Adhere the end to the roll with a tiny dab of glue. Pinch on opposite sides to form petals.

2. Cut one 8" (20.3 cm) strip from the yellow quilling paper. Roll using quilling tool to form the flower center.

3. Cut a 4" (10.2 cm) piece of the yellow quilling paper in half to form a ⅛" (3 mm) strip. Fold the 4" (10.2 cm) strip in varying length of five loops. Glue the bottom ends together and cut the folded looped ends open for the stamen.

4. Glue the petals to the yellow center. Use the slotted needle to curl the stamen ends.

5. Glue the stamen to the center to finish flower.

(continued)

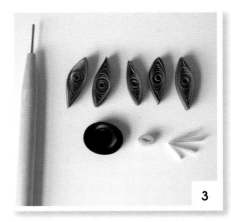

RED POPPY

1. Cut twenty 15" (38.1 cm) strips from the red quilling paper. Fold each strip into seven loops, graduating the lengths, as shown. Adhere the bottom ends together by dabbing glue, and cut the folded looped ends open. Insert one set into the center of another for each petal, creating either solid color or two tone petals.

2. Curl open ends using quilling tool to form shape.

3. Use red strips to wrap the petal three times. Cut remaining strip away and dab glue to hold in place. For two-toned look, use varying colors while wrapping the petals.

4. Pinch the top and two outer corners of each petal.

5. Adhere petals together to form flower shape. Roll a black strip into a roll and glue onto the center.

FOX GLOVE

1. Cut nine 12" (30.5 cm) strips from the two-tone quilling paper. Use the quilling tool to form strips into nine rolls.

2. Pinch one side to form teardrop shape. Glue to a green strip of quilling paper to form a bunch.

TO COMPLETE BOUQUET

1. Create leaves using same technique as in Red Marquise Flowers (page 133). Arrange flowers and leaves on a sheet of white cardstock, following the photo on page 132 or creating your own design. Glue the flowers to the frame. Try overlapping flowers to create dimension.

Quilled Rose
and Camellia Frame

QUILLED ROSE

1. Cut one 17" (43.2 cm) strip from the hot pink quilling paper. Slip the end of the strip into the slotted needle and roll several times to form center.

2. Fold the strip away at a slant and roll to form a petal. Keep the strip close at the bottom of the roll and allow the petal to flare. Stop when you reach the end of the fold.

3. Repeat step 2 to form more petals until desired size is reached. Glue the end in place.

(Continued)

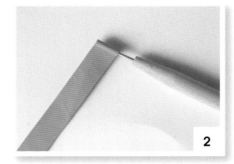

MATERIALS

* quilling paper, ½" (1.3 cm), hot pink and light pink
* quilling paper, ¼" (6 mm), yellow and light green
* craft glue
* scissors
* quilling tool
* plain white picture frame

QUILLED CAMELLIA

1. Cut a 3" (7.6 cm) strip from the yellow quilling paper. Cut fringes into the yellow strip.

2. Glue the strip to the pink strip.

3. Roll to form flower center.

4. Follow steps 2 and 3 for a making a Quilled Rose (page 135) to complete the Camellia.

TO COMPLETE THE FRAME

1. Cut five strips from the light green quilling paper and form loops.

2. Cut the loops open and curl ends to form scroll shapes.

3. Glue flowers and leaves onto frame as desired.

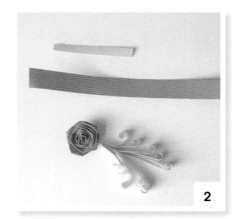

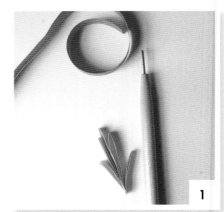

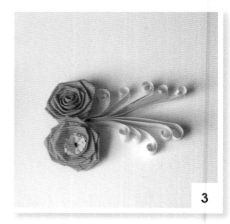

Quilled Dandelion

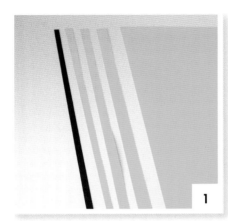

1.

1. Cut two ½" (1.3 cm) strips from the) yellow cardstock and a third strip measuring ¾" (1.9 cm). Taper the width of one of the yellow ½" (1.3 cm) strips to ¼" (6 mm) with scissors by cutting at a slant.

(continued)

MATERIALS

* cardstock, 70lb, or any lightweight paper, yellow and green, 12" x 12" (30.5 x 30.5 cm)
* stem wire, 18 gauge
* craft glue
* floral tape
* scissors
* quilting tool

2. Cut pointed fringes into all the strips with fine scissors.

3. Beginning at the narrow end, roll the tapered strip onto quilling tool to form center. Glue the end to the roll to keep it in place.

4. Add the remaining strips from narrowist to widest, to finish flowers, dabbing glue as you go along to secure in place.

5. Open out flower gently. Add green fringed strips to form sepals.

6. Glue taped stem wire onto flower head. Set aside to dry.

7. Cut two ½" (1.3 cm) strips of green cardstock. Fringe 2" (5.1 cm) of second strip, and glue onto first strip. Roll on quilling tool to form bud shape.

8. Form a bud center following instructions for flower center. Apply glue to the bottom, and push the center onto the green base, gently pushing out the green base to shape it. Add taped stem wire.

9. Using templates (page 157), cut out leaves from the green cardstock. Glue taped stem wire on the back of each leaf.

10. Arrange in pot.

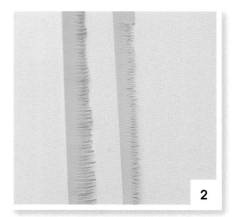

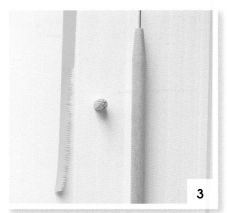

Quilled Sunflower

INSTRUCTIONS

1. Cut sixteen 17" (43.2 cm) strips of the yellow quilling paper. Follow steps 1–2 in Box Topper Flower (page 127) to make petals. Make similar petals in green for leaves.

2. Roll a brown strip using quilling tool to form center.

3. Glue the petals to the brown center, using eight on the first layer and eight more on top to form the flower.

4. Use a green strip to form an outline of the leaf and glue to the base to form shape. Add the green leaves to fill the outline. Add a green strip for the stem.

About the Author

FOR MARIA NOBLE, making flowers is a lifelong passion that began as a child watching her mother and aunt run a floral business. Using innovative methods, they made beautiful flowers from fabric, paper, and other materials for weddings and other special events. Maria started her own business ten years ago, incorporating her inherited skills and exploring ideas of her own to create new, distinctive flowers. The business has flourished, and now her exquisite flowers are sought out by consumers and businesses nationwide, including leading event planners in New York and Los Angeles. Her flowers have been featured in various magazines and on popular websites. Maria lives in Avon, Connecticut with her husband and two children.

Facebook: https://www.facebook.com/stjudescreations

Twitter: judepaperflower

Website: www.stjudescreations.com

Blog: http://stjudescreations.blogspot.com

Source List

Craft papers, florist wire, stem wires, and florist tape are available at major craft stores.

D. Blumchen and Company

www.blumchen.com

crepe paper folds

doublettte crepe paper

Castle In The Air

www.castleintheair.biz/shoppe/

crepe paper folds

doublettte crepe paper

florist crepe paper

New England Scrapbook Co.

www.newenglandscrapbook.com

specialty scrapbook paper

Whimsiquills

www.whimsiquills.com

quilling needles

quilling paper strips

Templates

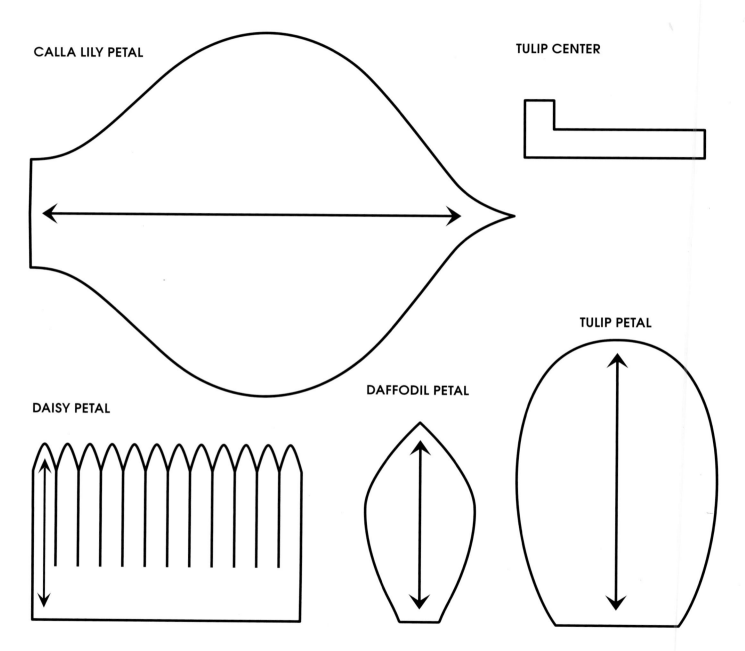

CALLA LILY PETAL

TULIP CENTER

TULIP PETAL

DAFFODIL PETAL

DAISY PETAL

100 Paper Flowers

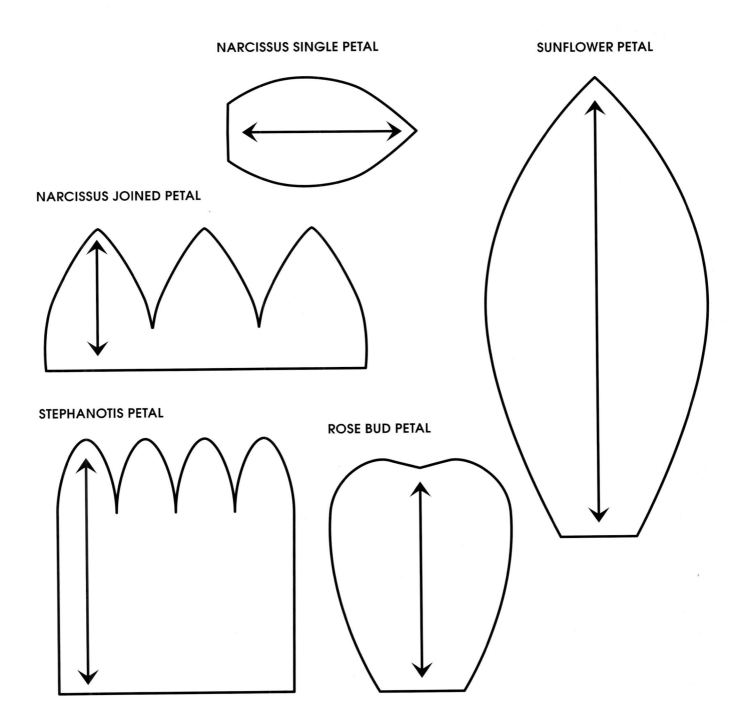

NARCISSUS SINGLE PETAL

SUNFLOWER PETAL

NARCISSUS JOINED PETAL

STEPHANOTIS PETAL

ROSE BUD PETAL

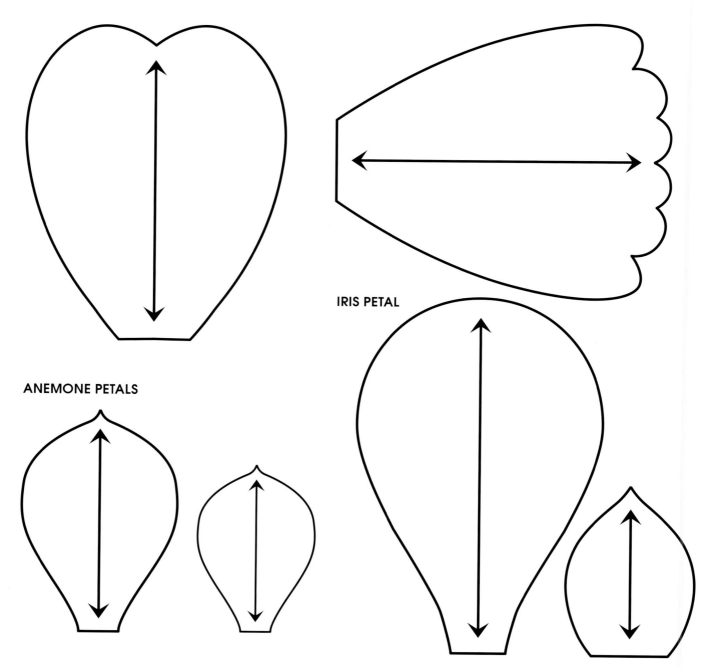

COUNTRY ROSE PETAL

PEONY SMALL PETAL

IRIS PETAL

ANEMONE PETALS

PEONY LARGE PETAL

LILY OF THE VALLEY LEAF

LILY OF THE VALLEY PETALS

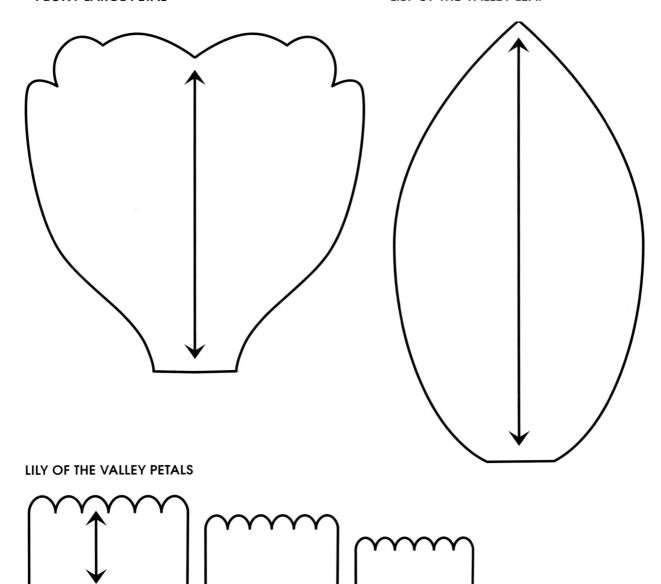

VIOLET PETAL

CAMELIA PETALS

ORANGE BLOSSOM PETAL AND LEAF

CRUSHED ROSE PETAL

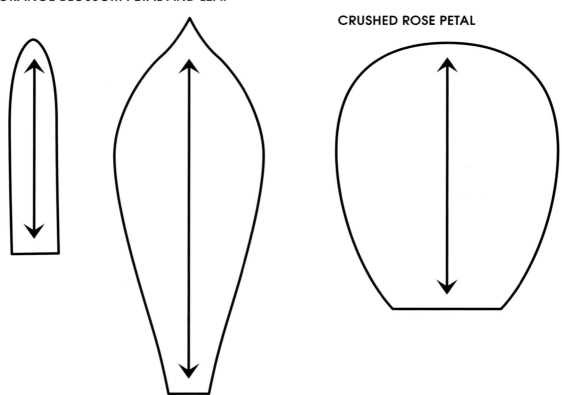

ORCHID PETALS

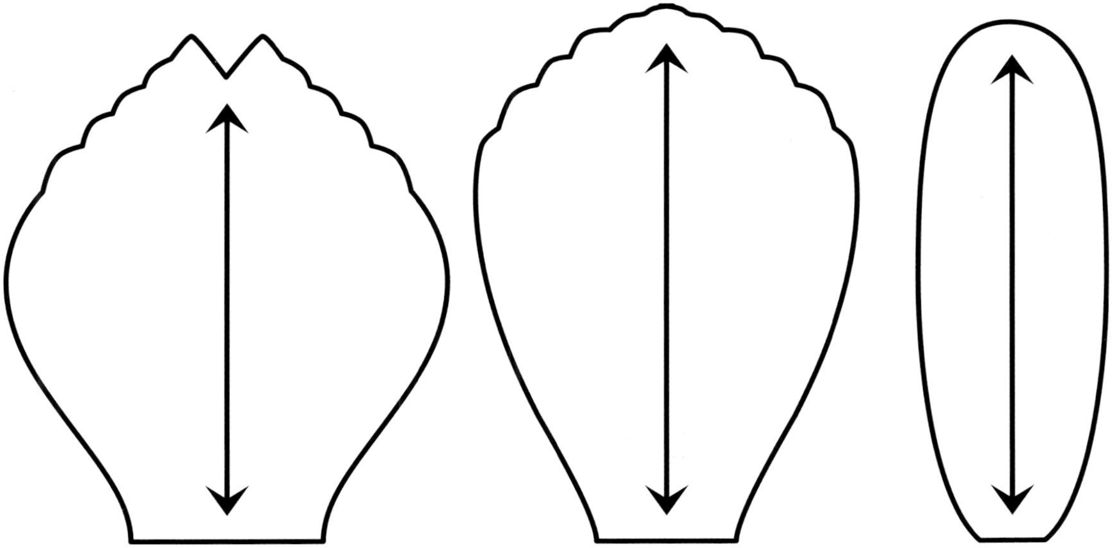

LILY PETAL

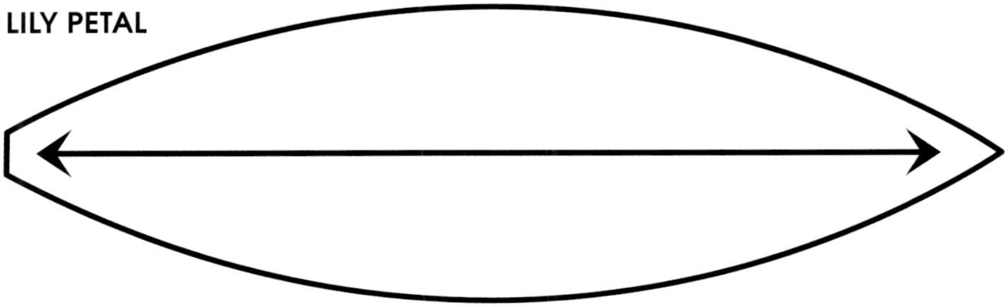

EASTER LILY PETAL

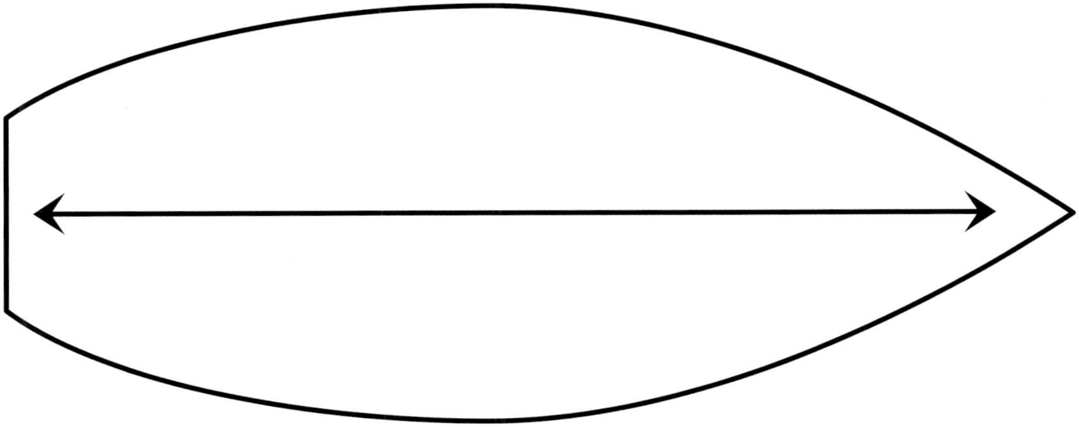

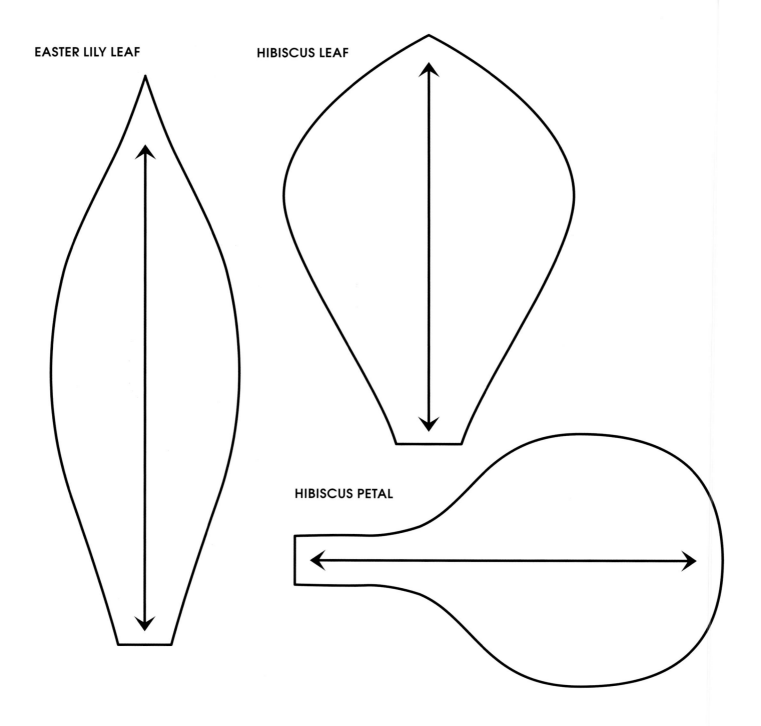

EASTER LILY LEAF

HIBISCUS LEAF

HIBISCUS PETAL

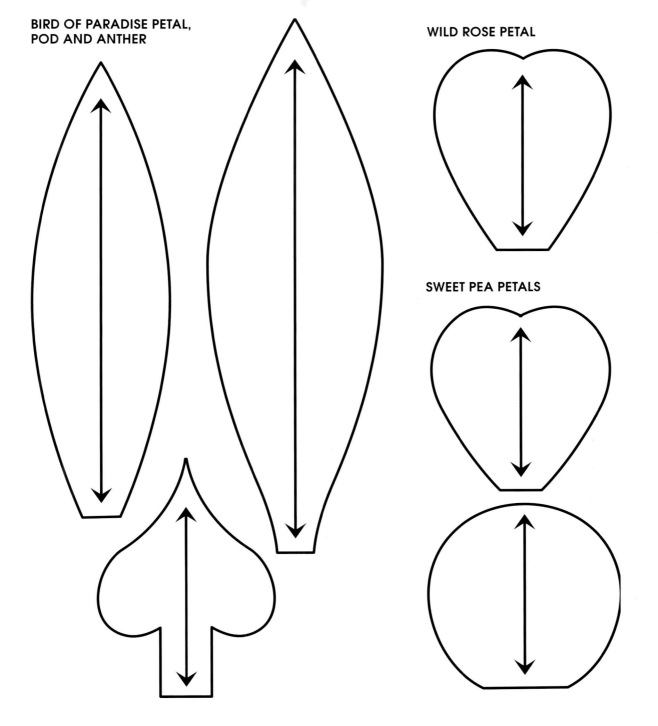

BIRD OF PARADISE PETAL,
POD AND ANTHER

WILD ROSE PETAL

SWEET PEA PETALS

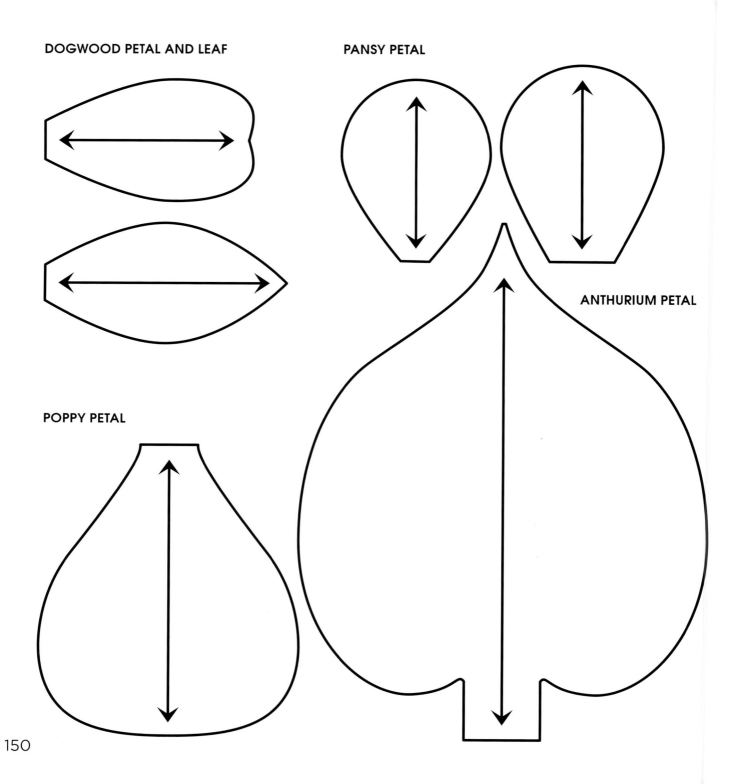

DOGWOOD PETAL AND LEAF

PANSY PETAL

POPPY PETAL

ANTHURIUM PETAL

150

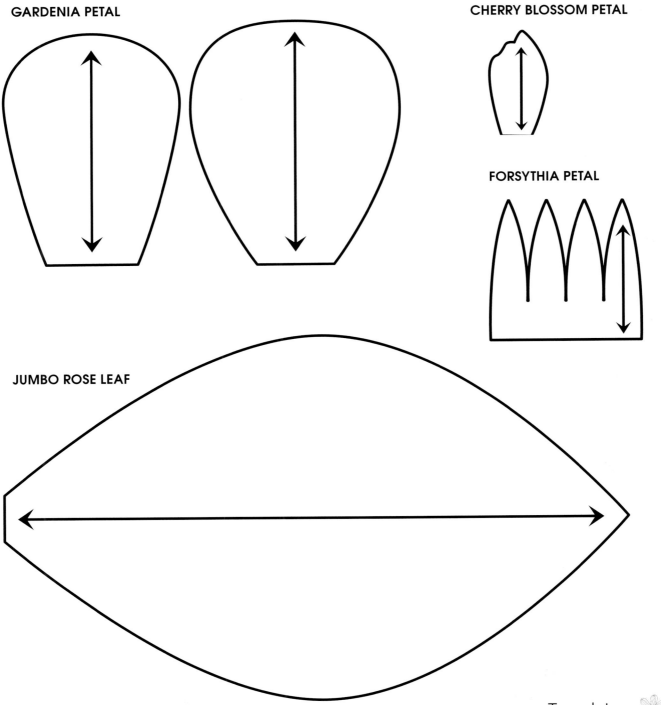

GARDENIA PETAL

CHERRY BLOSSOM PETAL

FORSYTHIA PETAL

JUMBO ROSE LEAF

JUMBO ROSE SMALL PETAL

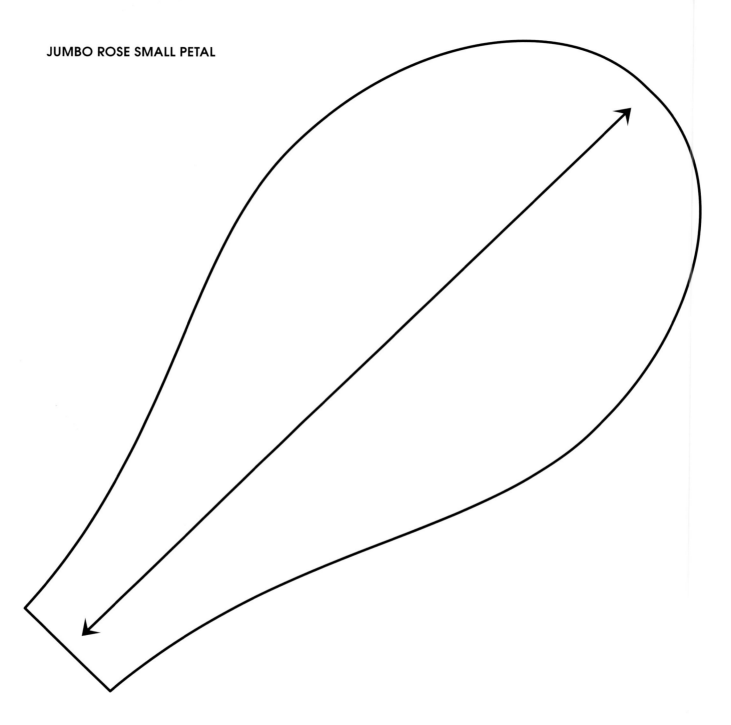

JUMBO ROSE LARGE PETAL

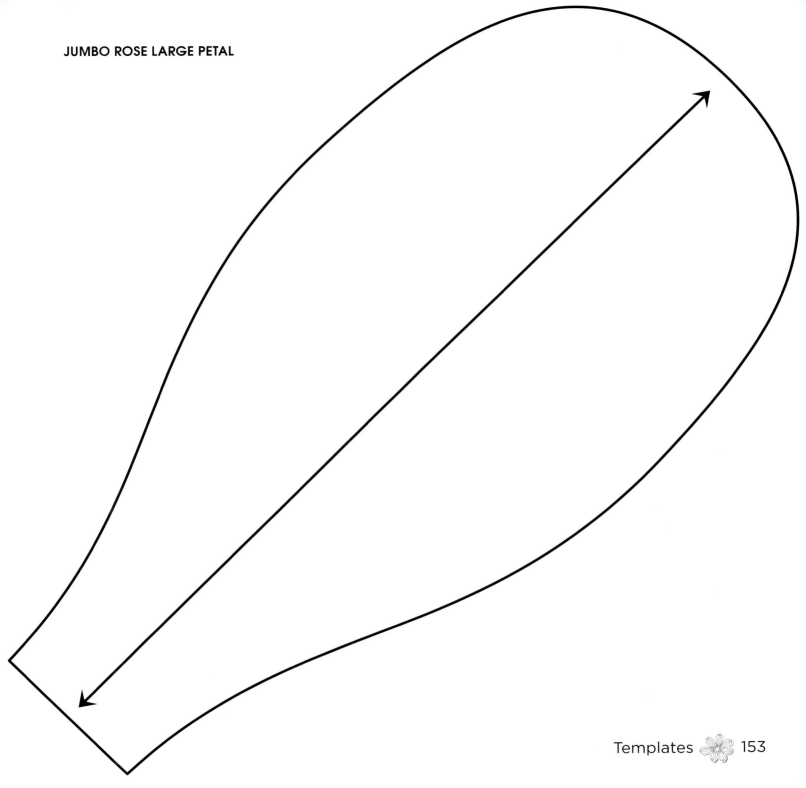

MAGNOLIA LEAF

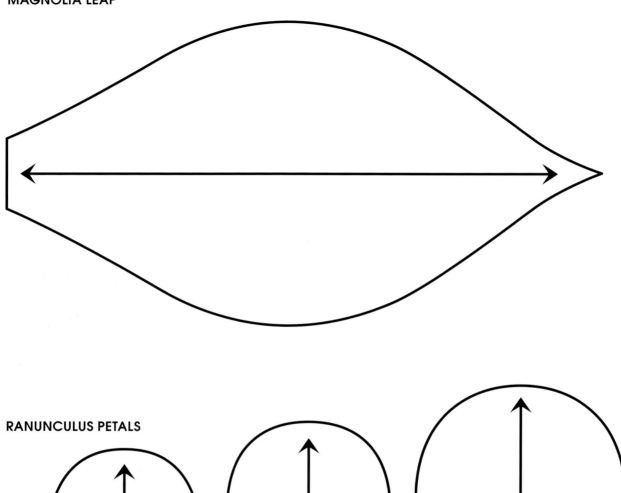

RANUNCULUS PETALS

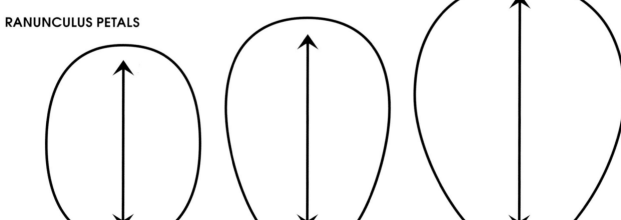

100 Paper Flowers

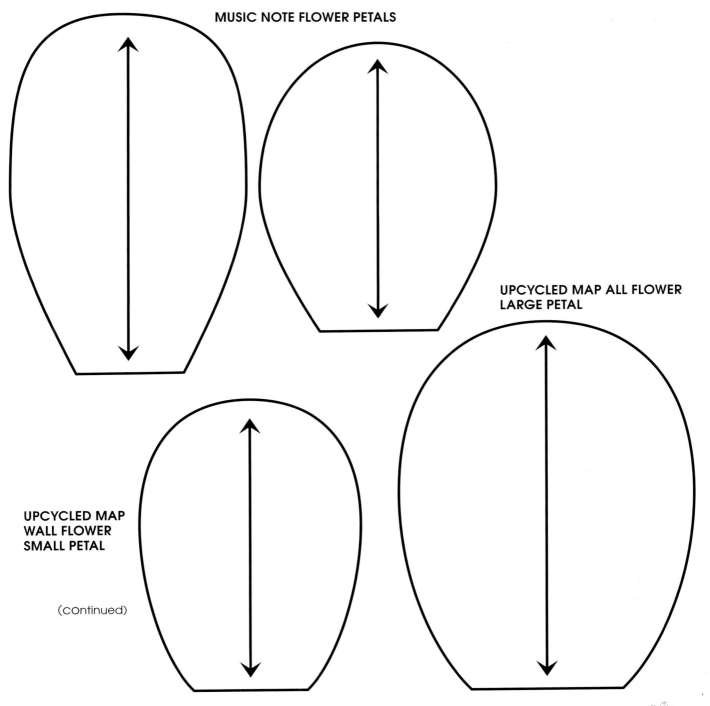

MUSIC NOTE FLOWER PETALS

UPCYCLED MAP ALL FLOWER
LARGE PETAL

UPCYCLED MAP
WALL FLOWER
SMALL PETAL

(continued)

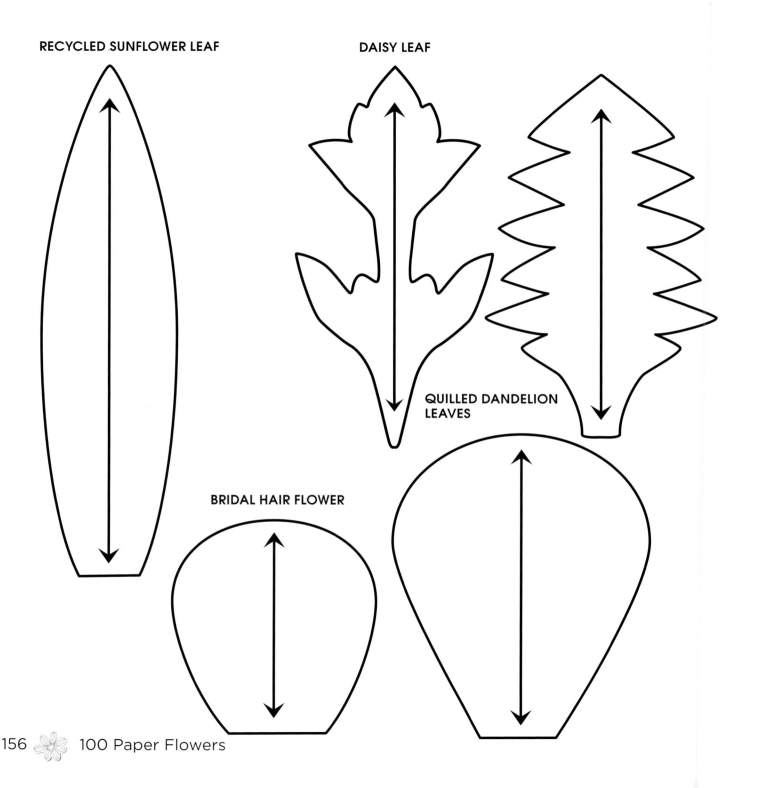

RECYCLED SUNFLOWER LEAF

DAISY LEAF

QUILLED DANDELION
LEAVES

BRIDAL HAIR FLOWER

RECYCLED SUNFLOWER PETAL

FIRE FLOWER PETAL

MAGNOLIA PETALS

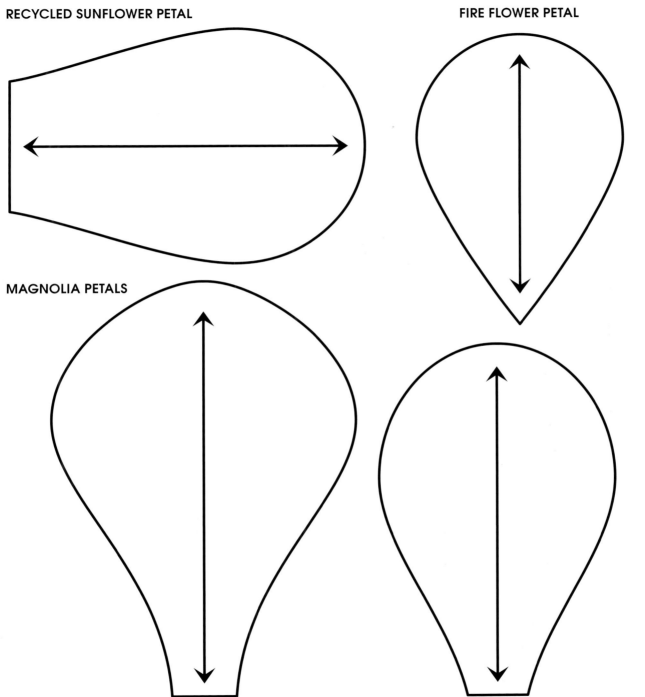

FANTASY FLOWER PETALS

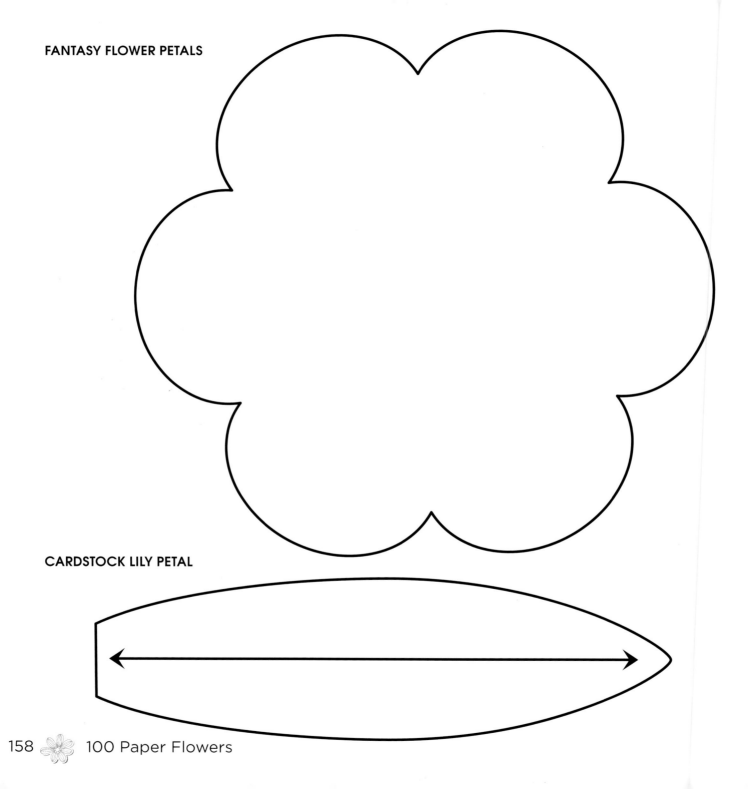

CARDSTOCK LILY PETAL

100 Paper Flowers

Don't miss the other book in the series!

Crochet 101
Deborah Burger
ISBN: 978-1-58923-752-0

More books on paper crafts!

Origami 101
Benjamin Coleman
ISBN: 978-1-58923-606-6

Playing with Paper
Helen Hiebert
ISBN: 978-1-59253-814-0

The Complete Photo Guide to Paper Crafts
Trice Boerens
ISBN: 978-1-58923-468-0

Art of Paper Quilling
Claire Sun-ok Choi
ISBN: 978-1-59253-386-2

Available online or at your local craft or book store.
www.CreativePub.com

Creative Publishing international

Our books are available as E-Books, too!
Many of our bestselling titles are now available as E-Books.
Visit **www.Qbookshop.com** to find links to e-vendors!